NEI KUNG

NEI KUNG

THE
SECRET TEACHINGS
OF THE
WARRIOR SAGES

KOSTA DANAOS

Inner Traditions
Rochester, Vermont

Inner Traditions International
One Park Street
Rochester, Vermont 05767
www.InnerTraditions.com

Library of Congress Cataloging-in-Publication Data

Danaos, Kosta.
     Nei Kung : the secret teachings of the warrior sages / Kosta Danaos.
          p. cm.
     ISBN 0-89281-907-3 (pbk.)
       1. Whispers from the Past—Metal—Microcosm—Spheres—
The thunderbolt—The Warrior elite—Practice—Wenwukuan Stories.
     2. Martial Arts.

GV1101 .D36 2002
796.8—dc 21

                                        2001006734

Printed and bound in the United States by Lake Book Manufacturing, Inc.

10 9 8 7 6 5 4 3

Text design and layout by Mary Anne Hurhula
This book was typeset in Weiss with OptiEve as the display typeface

CONTENTS

ACKNOWLEDGMENTS

I have had the great fortune in this life of being accepted as John Chang's apprentice; my efforts to reach the public would not have been possible without his consent and encouragement, and it is to him first and foremost that I must offer my gratitude. I have been blessed with people around me who make my path easier to walk, people who hold me steady when I am in danger of slipping; this book could not have been written without them. To Elias then, without whose support I would never have journeyed so far into the forgotten side of ourselves. To my students and friends at the Wenwukuan, many of whom train much more fiercely than I ever did; you are, each and every one of you, my brothers and sisters. To Handoko, without whose assistance neither *The Magus of Java* nor *Nei Kung* would have been possible. To Karolos, for all the sojourns into humanity's past and the training we do together. And finally to Doris, for putting up with me; it can't be easy.

INTRODUCTION

There was once a man in China who liked pictures of dragons. His clothing and his furniture were therefore accordingly adorned with dragons. This deep affection for their kind was brought to the attention of the Dragon Lord, who one day sent a real dragon to stand outside the man's window. It is said that he promptly died of fright.

Yamamoto Tsunetomo[1]

Each of us lives within the confines of our individual reality. This is our choice; we *choose* to live in such a manner—with the same beliefs of what is real and what is not as those often dictated to us from birth. Our society certainly exerts its influence on our behavior, limiting us within its predefined systems and within what it perceives as common sense. Few people are above this. Our dreams, however, unrestricted by society's whims and the binding chains of narrow logic, often soar above these confines. We are then exposed to a different reality, a place where our innermost hopes and desires are free to express themselves. You see, we have nothing to lose in this new reality. We tell ourselves, "This is just a dream," and so are free to live as we truly wish. Protected by our private curtains, free from

---

1. From Hagakure (*Hidden in the Leaves*), written by Yamamoto Tsunetomo in 1716, which, through the patronage of Mishima Yukio, has come to be known as *The Book of the Samurai*. It has recently been made popular again in the West by Jim Jarmusch's movie *Ghost Dog*.

retribution, we dance out our hopes and aspirations, our innermost fears, within our own minds.

As a species, we have not always been so submissive. Primitive man was free to explore his world without the constraints of a rigorously mechanized society to bind him; he was free to investigate his earth and discern its shape without preconception. The realm of dreams and that of the physical were not so far apart; indeed, the shaman, whose job it was to sojourn into the world of dreams and twilight, was an integral component of society. One could say that primitive man used his dreams as an extension of his five better-known senses. Even today, however, the dreams that dance in our subconscious mind can take shape in the physical world. Progressing as we do through life, we frequently come to find that the myths and legends of humanity, the stories our grandmothers told us, are indeed true. And then what? What do you do when a myth presents itself to you in the flesh? What do you do when a quaint folk belief, accepted by your ancestors but denied by our modern day, knocks at your door? Do you run away? Do you have a heart attack and collapse?

I myself do not. Never having used drugs and being healthy in all respects, I do not doubt the testimony of my own senses. I do not run away. I do not hide. Nor am I afraid, for fear of ridicule, to share with others the revelations I unearth. Part of me is a warrior, you see, and loves a good fight—and as anyone who has given one knows, an academic presentation often turns into a good fight, played with the mind rather than with the fists, and against multiple adversaries at that.

Welcome then, once again, to my world. It is a place where there are no limits, where whatever once had shape and form in the history of humanity has found a home. My world revolves around that forgotten part of our soul—that forgotten side of ourselves—that has been trod upon for reasons of control and domination, I believe, for the last four millennia of our development. What exactly is the forgotten side of ourselves? It is that portion of our heritage that is scoffed at as superstition or make-believe today. It is that part of our innermost being that quietly acknowledges aspects of reality we know to be true, yet hesitates to openly acknowledge them for fear of ridicule. It is our inner connection to those archetypal aspects of existence that primitive or less "modern" cultures continue to embrace, but that we Westerners look upon as quaint, or backward, or even as (shudder) "neat."[2] It is that side of ourselves that exists with open access to all that may defy our world's ideas of logic and reason.

In 1994 I saw a documentary on television that changed my life forever. Called *Ring of Fire: East of Krakatoa,* and produced by the brothers Lorne and Lawrence Blair in 1988, the film described their experiences in the Indonesian archipelago. Central to the documentary was a brief sequence with a shy and somewhat reclusive Chinese-Javanese acupuncturist who performed wonderful things, unbelievable things, for the camera. He demonstrated his full mastery of the phenomenon of *ch'i,* or bioenergy, by generating an "electrical" current within his body, which he used first to heal one filmmaker of an eye infection, and then to set a newspaper on fire with his hand.

Ring of Fire caused thousands to seek out this individual in pursuit of instruction; I was one of the successful ones. In the book *The Magus of Java,* I described my initial encounter with this master, whose true identity I have hidden behind the pseudonym John Chang (though John really is his name, and so is Chang, after a fashion).[3] After many trials and tribulations, he finally accepted me as his student, and I have since been privileged enough to witness phenomena that most people can only dream of. In my years of study with John Chang, I have experienced pyrogenesis, telekinesis, levitation, telepathy, and

---

2. This inner conviction that myths have a basis in reality is why comic books and films are filled with stories and pictures depicting the fantastic. We cannot reject what is in the end a part of our own evolution.

3. I have been berated by my peers in the Mo-Pai for several decisions I made in writing *The Magus of Java,* not the least of which was my choice of the spelling Chang for our teacher's name. The actual spelling, as the Chinese-Javanese use it, of that particular portion of his Chinese name is Djiang. However, I thought that Chang would be more familiar to Westerners and easier to pronounce, if slightly phonetically different. In any case, for reasons of historical accuracy he has allowed me to reveal parts of his real Chinese name: His family name is Ie and his middle name is Djiang. He has adopted the Christian name John, however I am not at liberty to reveal his Indonesian surname. This "secrecy" is part of a continuing effort to protect his privacy. I trust and hope that you will understand.

things even more exotic. I have spoken with spirits and can testify to their reality. Equally important, I have learned my own teacher's story, and have been given permission to publish it. John Chang is a direct heir to the lineage of the sixth-century B.C.E. sage Mo Tzu, who was Confucius's greatest rival. His discipline, called the Mo-Pai, was, until now, little known in the West.

The method through which these incredible abilities are arrived at is called, in Chinese, *nei kung*, or "inner power." It is the equivalent of the Hindu-Buddhist practice of kundalini yoga, though nei kung involves a martial art and martial practice. Central to the discipline is the transformation of sexual energy into pure unadulterated power, a force that the practitioner can use at will. The "cauldron" in which this formidable elixir is brewed is called the *dantien* (elixir field) in Chinese, and is a bioenergetic nexus located four fingers below our navel.

This second book of mine, in many ways part two of *The Magus of Java*, is not so much about my master, though you will find him weaving himself in and out of these pages. Rather, this book is about how his teaching opened my mind and senses and enabled me to perceive the forgotten side of ourselves. It is by far a more scholarly— and more practical—book than the first one. This is a study guide written for those who were excited enough by *The Magus of Java* to pursue further instruction (though I am hoping it will stand on its own as a literary effort) and for those who, regardless of their familiarity with *The Magus of Java*, wish to learn more about nei kung.

As I have grown in my knowledge of the Mo-Pai tradition, I have discovered that teachings similar to those of the Mo-Pai once had a home all around the world; I have found evidence of nei kung techniques and references to yin and yang energy in almost every ancient culture examined by modern archaeology. It would seem that these teachings endured in China as fossilized versions of what was once universal in distribution. My ambition, then, is that they once again find a home in every country, in every city, in every small village around the globe. I hope to begin with you, the reader; I hope to convince you, through these pages, to undertake a regular meditative discipline, a regimen whose scope you may choose at will and tailor to your own personality and aspirations. For it is meditation, in the end, that is the key that opens the door to the forgotten side of ourselves.

I fear we have become unbearably arrogant, you see. Confident as gods in the technological progress we have made, we scoff at the men and women who were our ancestors. Oh, we admire the Pyramids, the Parthenon, the Great Wall of China. We marvel at the cave drawings and sculptured bison in the Paleolithic caves of France. We delight in achievements and say, "I wonder how they managed that with the technology of their time." In essence, we are patronizing them; we consider ourselves superior. We deny the full spectrum of what they themselves believed in. We do not seek to understand them, these people who were our forefathers; we do not seek to discover why they made the choices they did, what they had seen, what knowledge they possessed that was different from our own. It is from our own standpoint that we try to reach them, ever judgmental. We deny their world, and try to refashion and study it based on our own. What nonsense!

People are ever practical, especially under conditions where survival is an issue, and life in earlier times was something one had to struggle for on an almost daily basis. Ancient peoples, then, cultivated belief because they saw that there was pragmatic gain in doing so. Since having been accepted as John Chang's student, it dawned on me that every myth and legend of humanity probably has a basis somewhere in fact. For example, for centuries scholars thought that Homer's Troy was a myth, a story concocted by a blind poet—until a German merchant with more pathos than scientific knowledge stumbled onto her ruins through sheer persistence. John Chang's paranormal abilities are real; thousands of people throughout the world can step forward and testify to that fact. How many other myths and legends are true, hidden in the leaves, silent and waiting for a dedicated seeker to find?

I cannot speak for all of them, though I would like to believe that there are *yeti* and four-hundred-year-old *yogis* living in the Himalayan mountains, as I have been told by Tibetan monks. I personally believe in all manner of spirits, ghosts, and goblins—yes, sometimes it is our nightmares that take shape as well. But meeting such beings is not easy or common; the odds are one in ten thousand or more. Usually, our imagination gets carried away, influenced as it is by cinema and literature, and we believe that something extraordinary is happening when in fact our subconscious mind is tricking us.

Ultimately, we believe in the fantastic because we *want* to believe, because we have a *need* to believe; the forgotten side of ourselves is ever awake within us, calling to us from fields of dreams. Because our consumer-oriented society has made life mundane and stripped the magic from our existence, we desperately desire an alternative. Social precepts, for the present, however, dictate that we must ignore these whispers of our past, that we must continue to forget that part of ourselves. In truth, it would be just as easy for an individual to saw off an arm or a leg caught in a trap. This part of ourselves is written into our DNA; we cannot walk away from it. In the end, ignoring our innermost voice leads to desperation, and it is this desperation that proves to be our undoing, for once desperate, we are no longer pragmatic in our pursuits. Not being practical is dangerous—knowledge accumulated over millennia becomes trivialized and people wind up living in fairy tales.

In truth, finding our forgotten side is not easy and often requires the fortitude of a warrior. It can be frightening—compound this natural phobia with the added factor of a multitude of frauds and hucksters preying on the innocent and you will understand that you must tread very, very carefully. In the Orient, where masters secretly coexisted with Western-style development until this past generation, things were much easier to discern: While there were many frauds, true masters were known by reputation and were widely respected. The regularly accepted practice of challenge-matches saw to this—frauds were afraid to raise their ugly heads for dread of being challenged by a true master. Today, duels being rigorously frowned upon by the legal system, this is no longer the case, and even in the East, prospective students must be ever wary of clever swindlers. The forgotten side of ourselves is, in short, dangerous turf, and requires a very special type of individual to traverse; this person must be willing first and foremost to face him- or herself—and most people shy away from just that.

I cannot speak for every myth, for every circumstance that each of us may have encountered; I can only speak for myself. In fact, each of us, in the end, speaks only for ourselves. This book, then, is my personal journey, my individual sojourn into the forgotten side. Please enjoy it. In some places the text may seem complex and some pieces may seem to hang separately from others, but I encourage you to stick with it—I have two reasons for presenting this book in its chosen format. The first is that I want to impart to the reader a portrait of what my life and training, and those of my students and friends, are like in my native Greece. Of its own nature, painting such a portrait is a complex task. The second is that I am obligated by vows I have given to teach cryptically, and so am laying out pieces of the puzzle as I go along. It is up to the reader to assemble these pieces into the larger picture; I hope each and every one of you is successful.

Finally, I return to the dragon mentioned at the very beginning of this introduction. Desiring something and finding it are two altogether different things, coming to terms with a miracle another matter entirely. This is where fortitude of spirit exhibits itself. Should a dragon, then, happen to come along on a bright morning to stand politely outside your window, his scales glistening in the sun, don't be afraid. Rather, invite him in for tea. You will never forget the experience, and may be surprised to discover that he will enjoy your company as well. I believe, in the end, that dragons and their like miss us almost as much as we miss them.

Chapter 1

WHISPERS FROM
THE PAST

. . . o'er Delphi's long deserted shrine,
where, save that feeble fountain,
all is still.

George Gordon, Lord Byron

I was standing on a mountaintop, screaming up at God.

Six years had passed since I met the Magus of Java, John Chang of the Mo-Pai, and had been accepted as his student. Six years, and during that time my life had changed completely. I had become a much wiser and well-balanced person, of that there could be no doubt. But I was also a much more somber individual than I had been. There is nothing like ignorance to keep a man happy. I had dispensed with it in search of knowledge and was paying the price—life was a constant struggle between old cravings and new yearnings. The path followed by my master was a difficult one and would make my own life austere should I choose to follow it to completion.

When I first started the Mo-Pai training I had all the enthusiasm of the neophyte and that ardor had carried me along for many years. It was after advancing rapidly along the path that I faltered for the first time, and picked myself up, and walked farther, and faltered again. I came to realize that all such disciplines are, in the end, motivated by one of two things: either a profound love for God or a profound hatred for a given individual or group of individuals. There seemed to be little room to maneuver between these two extremes. The training is very difficult and unending; it required withdrawing from society, if only in part, to be able to meditate and perform the necessary psychophysical energetics. Nei kung training operates on the molecular level and actually modifies the DNA of the trainee. It is dangerous and demanding—you must sacrifice material ambitions for the sake of spiritual ones. There is no way around this.

I didn't know how to handle it. As for my motivations, my feelings for God were mixed and I didn't really hate anyone so terribly. I was stuck in the middle, wondering what quirk of destiny had set me on this path.

Continuously harnessing my sexuality was no great joy, either, and much of nei kung centers on changing sexual energy to spiritual and physical power. I had no pretensions about not liking society and everything in it. A pretty girl will always turn my head, I like to drink and smoke cigars, and I can spend whole days slothfully watching television. In truth, I am lazy by nature and hate getting up in the morning. All in all, hardly the stereotype of the dedicated yogi, you will agree. But the training wouldn't let me go. It ran my life, and there was no escaping it.

"I want to sell everything I own, turn my ancestral home in the mountains into a hotel, and live and train up there for the rest of my life," I advised John during one of my trips to Indonesia.

"If you had told me that last month, I would have said go ahead and do it," he said. "But now, I don't know."

"Why not?"

"Last week I went into meditation and asked my master[1] why none of my students had managed to combine yin and yang in their dantien[2] and finish Level Four."

Grandmaster Liao, John Chang's teacher, had died in 1962, but

1. Liao Tzu Tong, the deceased past master of the Mo-Pai (my *sigung*, or "grandfather-teacher"). The reader will have to refer to *The Magus of Java* for details.
2. The major energy center of the body, located four fingers below the navel.

his consciousness was still accessible to my own master somewhere beyond space-time.

"What did he say?"

"He said that this level of power is a gift granted by such laws as govern the Universe, and is not subject to individual human will. It is a part of a person's aura."

I was silent. John sensed my question.

"At the deepest level, there are really only three kinds of aura," he continued, "white, black, and yellow. These colors reflect the innermost essence of our being. A white aura is that of a soul who is good at heart, a black aura is of one who is evil in the end. A yellow aura is that of a person who is at complete peace with the Universe. In our school, one must have attained this tranquillity to pass on to Level Four." He paused. "In other lineages, this is not always the case." John shook himself, as if an unpleasant thought had invaded his privacy. I was tempted to ask, but stood quiet instead.

"In each generation, Kosta," he continued, "only one student has become like I am—at least until now."

My breath caught in my throat. "What color is my aura?" I blurted out without a hint of subtlety.

"I don't know." He raised a hand to silence my protest. "I can see the deepest color of your aura only when I am at full power, during the times when I am training in the mountains. Not now."

My heart dropped. "It can't be me

"Why not?"

"Because I'm already forty years old!" I growled. "It should be someone who is a kid now, so that . . ."

"You're *not* old," he snapped, "and people live a lot longer now than they used to. They'll have great need for wisdom combined with power in the future, believe me. Besides, events seem to suggest that in this generation the power may go to the West."

"What?"

"Yes—the Chinese are less appreciative of their own culture than they used to be. Perhaps the next master of the Mo-Pai will be a Westerner. Or maybe a young Chinese boy residing in a Western nation. But he will be a "citizen of the world," of that I am sure."

I was speechless.

"Who knows?" he slapped me on the back. "It may even be an old man like you. Liao Sifu has certainly taken an interest in you."

I had had run-ins with the Grandmaster's spirit; on two separate instances I had been the victim of his practical jokes. Playing straight man to a supernatural comedian with godlike powers was no fun.

That conversation had torn me in two, leaving doubt to gnaw at my soul. When I was younger, I dreamed of becoming a fighter pilot, but failed the eye exam. There was nothing I could do—no effort on my part could help me overcome a congenital deficiency in circumstances where rigid standards were necessary. Likewise in nei kung training there are prerequisites that must be met in order to advance. Failing to meet these, it is best not to be overly ambitious. Could I accomplish the training? And if I couldn't develop abilities like John's, would I at least manage to complete the Third Level of Power in this lifetime?

I resolved to die trying. Wherever I turned, I ran into constraints imposed by God or Fate or Jodo (in Chinese, "the will of heaven"), constraints that got my temper going whenever I brooded over them. Being by blood a Greek (though by culture a Hellenistic Greek), divine restraints ran against the grain. You have only to read from Greek mythology to see that it portrays a constant struggle of man against his gods. The Titan Prometheus, who had risked the wrath of heaven to bring fire to mankind, was my own personal role model. I decided to emulate him. Rather than a profound love for God, it was an extreme devotion to mankind and nature that fueled my efforts.

But the gods always won in the end, damn it. I felt like a bonsai that has the soul of a mighty oak of the wild, but, through the desire and shaping of a superior force, is constrained by wires to be a servant and pet destined to live out its life in a pot.

I had many decisions to make, and there could be no compromises. I had come to realize why Liao Sifu had been so austere with my own master—which was why I was standing on top of a mountain, screaming up at God. I had come to spend a full month in retreat in the wild, living in a shack that one of my students had built in the middle of nowhere, far away from society and its temptations. My only companions were foxes, rabbits, mice, snakes, scorpions, flies, mosquitoes, and the occasional wolf.

And an earth-spirit or seven, but more on that later.

I wanted to know what God wanted from me. I was tired of living with ambiguity. I was forty years old, fed up, and the message I was sending upward was, "Either give me clear direction, or leave me alone!" This particular bonsai wasn't feeling very aesthetically pleasing at the moment—and I was angry with the Deity for giving me this particular shape and task.

But there was no question that I was developing. I had begun to feel peoples' emotions in an almost uncanny manner. Many times I was able to sense the thoughts uppermost in their minds as well. There was nothing mystical about the experience. In fact, my own students who were training for Level One disclosed similar abilities. Telepathy between us became routine. One student dreamed that I had entered his room and was having a conversation with him. He was shocked when I repeated the words we had exchanged—I had seen the same thing at the same instant while in meditation!

My martial arts skills improved greatly. Upon testing the energy content of one of my students whose name is Stamatis, John showed us that I had at least five times that man's energy. He did so by passing a current of 1 percent of his total power through his forearm. My student could not touch my master's arm, while I grasped it comfortably. Later I found that I could then stand 2 percent of John's power, while Stamatis could comfortably tolerate 0.40 percent. I had five times my student's bioenergy! As a result, I had to practice very carefully in the training hall, keeping the ch'i down in the dantien where it belonged. But every so often it crept up, and people went flying. I had heard of a brother student in the United States, James, who could no longer touch his own students while training, for fear of sending them to the hospital.

And things began to be revealed to me; the Universe opened up and showed me its secrets. My personality had undergone a radical transformation; I was a potpourri of ideas, knowledge, impressions, and experiences from the standpoint of Eastern and Western science.

I no longer had a specific belief system, for example, either as a scientist or with regard to religion, and I took nothing for granted. I understood that those precepts that we blindly accept as truth today are merely temporary axioms, and tomorrow they may be laughed at and criticized. I became aware that time tends to equalize all things and lifts the veils from some of them, and I was beginning to understand its flow, the way the Universe works, the Tao.

I was really miserable. As I said, there is nothing like ignorance to make a man feel safe. To better understand the future, I began to study the past. I learned that what John was now teaching me had been discovered, experienced, and categorized by many diverse ethnic groups throughout the centuries, foremost among them being my own ancestors. There is nothing new under the sun.

POLES OF FOREVER

There are two principal forces that make up our Universe—the Chinese call them yin and yang. These two energies oppose each other continuously, locked in eternal combat. The yin is the primal chaos that existed before our own space-time was created. It is beyond form and function, incomprehensible to us and yet an essential part of our being. Gravity, for example, is part of the yin field, as are black holes, as are our very souls. Yin is vibration, the interstellar cold of outer space; it is winter and night, sleep and water. And yet sleep and water are a necessary part of life; without them, we die.

The yang energy is solar fire, the driving force that opposes gravity and creates space-time. Without this contrasting dynamism, the force of gravity would have long ago collapsed all matter in the Universe into one huge, solitary black hole, in essence ending creation. It is the yang force of solar nuclear fusion that propels space and time and first enabled us to live in the form we have now. The yang fuels our lives; it is the positive that gives direction, the light that drives away the darkness, the sum and substance that gives us joy. (Please see appendix 2.)

And yet the yang by itself would kill us just as a man unprotected in the desert will soon die of exposure. It is only when it is balanced with the opposing yin that life thrives and has meaning. This unquestionable axiom—yang must be balanced by yin—is an indication that the Universe has been created with intent, and that this intent was none other than the creation of life.

These two energies were omnipresent in all ancient cultures. The Chinese spoke of yin and yang, the Tibetans of the red drop and the white drop, the ancient Greeks of chaos and order, the Navajo of Mother Earth and Father Sky. We can see their entwining energies in depictions of Hindu and Buddhist chakras, in Mesopotamian religious imagery, in the ancient Greek *caduceus* of Hermes, and, perhaps, in the DNA strand itself. The code of these two energies is cosmic and timeless; they are a reality that all accomplished human cultures have stumbled upon.

According to the Mo-Pai tradition, there are seventy-two Levels of Power that make up the steps to ultimate enlightenment, the greatest point of human existence. That much I had learned from John Chang. Mention of these levels is universal. The Sufis say that there are 72,000 veils between God and man. Hindu yogis talk about either the seventy-two chakras of the human body or the 72,000 *nadi* that must be opened before the thousand-petalled lotus blooms.

All these levels have to do with yin and yang. On their own, our spirits are yin, a series of vibrations, standing waves inscribed in the medium of the yin field. Like a computer program on a CD, our very essence is nothing more than a "subroutine" in the energies of the primal chaos. As soon as we enter space and time and become yang, this vibration in the yin field takes form. In fact, it replicates itself fractally, taking shape first in our DNA and then, through our DNA, in our human bodies. It is similar to inserting a CD into a personal computer and calling up a program, only to watch it materialize on the screen.[3]

---

3. I will expand on this theory in later chapters.

As spiritual beings we become more powerful, more self-aware, when we manage to combine the two energies, yin and yang, *inside the zero nodes* of this standing wave, finally reaching ultimate enlightenment when they reach the very top of our head. It is like filling up a glass: You start at the bottom and work your way up.

The method followed by the Mo-Pai is millennia-old and very effective. You begin by filling up the body's "energy warehouse" with solar energy, in Chinese, *yang ch'i*. This warehouse, the dantien (elixir field), is located four fingers below the navel. Called the *hara* in Japanese, it has been written about profusely in the last fifty years, and there is no need to elaborate on it here. If you imagine this energy center as a sphere, you could assume that it would be empty at Level Zero, and full of yang energy at the end of Level One:

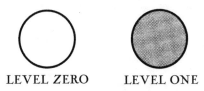

LEVEL ZERO   LEVEL ONE

Fig. 1. The dantien is empty at Level Zero (left) and full of yang energy at the end of Level One (right).

Accomplishing this is no easy task, because the only way to do so is exclusively through meditation. You must be in *actual* meditation, a condition similar to the borderline between sleep and waking, for eighty-one hours in order to fill the dantien. When the typical practitioner attempts meditation, he actually achieves it for only three minutes during every hour of sitting. Therefore, completing Level One can require 1,620 hours of sitting in the meditative posture. At an hour a day, it would take the average man four-and-a-half years to conclude this stage of the training.

Following the completion of Level One, the student begins compressing the yang ch'i in his dantien, in essence making it "hard." This
is accomplished through breath retention and specific movements. A
graphic representation would look like this:

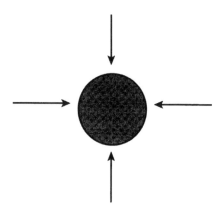

Fig. 2. Compressing yang ch'i in the dantien

It is difficult. Our bodies have only so much energy, and we use
that energy to compress the yang ch'i in our dantien. You have to be
strong to do this training. Push too hard, and you drain away your
very life force while trying to progress. Train too little, and you get
nowhere. It is a matter of balance and requires patience, consistency,
and perseverance.

And the third level is even harder. We have said that the yin and
yang energies are opposing forces. The student who finishes Level
Two has enough yang energy in his dantien to begin "snapping" the
restraints holding the dantien in place, using the power of the stored
and compressed yang. It is, in essence, like tugging hard to snap
a piece of twine. The dantien is held in place by five cords that have
a correlation in both the physical (yang) and spiritual (yin) realms.
We can imagine them as strings, four on one plane diagonally
opposing each other, and one center string perpendicular to those.
To break the confines of the yin field you must break these strings
one by one and, in doing so, allow the dantien (by then a hardened

ball of compressed yang) to move around inside the body. When a student cuts the first four strings, he completes Level Three;[4] graphically, it might look something like this:

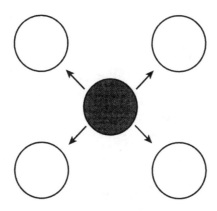

Fig. 3. The completion of Level Three: cutting the first four cords holding the dantien and breaking the confines of the yin field

This is the peak that most people can hope for. Finishing Level Three endows the practitioner with superior abilities. Level Three students cannot be cut with a knife when aware of the blow. I have personally witnessed a pellet from an air rifle fired at point blank range ricochet off the flesh of one brother student who had reached Level Three. Startling those at this level is dangerous, for their ch'i is governed by their emotions and flies to protect them. I have heard of three separate instances where students at Level Three killed the muggers who tried to assault them, despite their best intentions to

---

4. From a strict genealogical and historic standpoint, the definitions of the levels of power I have given here and in *The Magus of Java* are inaccurate. In the Mo-Pai we speak of Level One pretty much as described, then lower Level Two and upper Level Two (in which four of the cords are cut), which leads to Level Three (where only the central cord is still attached) and Level Four. The description I used in my books is less confusing, and the reader should stick to the terminology provided unless he or she becomes a "closed door" Mo-Pai disciple.

restrain their power. Their hardened ch'i, governed by the emotions of men protecting their own lives, had blown out the aggressors' hearts; cursory investigations at hospitals simply showed that each of these men had died of a heart attack.

I myself am always wary around brother students who are at a higher level, and make sure never to surprise them when we are training together.

Those at Level Three have other powers beyond this physical strength and a degree of physical invulnerability. When the strings of karma are cut, each student develops a particular ability according to his own psychophysical makeup. One man might be able to see six months into the future; another can heal various illnesses with his touch. There are no rules that govern this gift; it is up to Jodo, the will of heaven.

Beyond this point, only those with a yellow aura can progress to Level Four. These fortunates sever the last thread—the fifth—mooring the dantien and send their yang down to meet the yin that flows into their bodies through the perineum. After a time, the two energies rise together like lovers. The student yogi then seizes them by force of will and squeezes them into the vestibule of his dantien, where they coexist as *t'ai chi*, the Supreme Ultimate. There, in the dantien, they look like this:

Fig. 4. T'ai chi: yin and yang together in the dantien at the end of Level Four

The fortunate yogi who accomplishes t'ai chi has harnessed the lightning, and as such has power over space-time. He has sixty-eight more levels to progress through before achieving complete enlightenment, that pinnacle of human existence. At that point, the crown chakra at the very top of the head opens and the yogi completes Level Seventy-Two.

In the entire history of China, only two people have achieved this state. One was Bodhidharma, the Indian (perhaps Persian?) prince who taught Ch'an (Zen) Buddhism and kung fu at the Shaolin temple. The other was Chang San Feng of the Wutang-Pai, credited by many as the creator of *t'ai chi chuan*, and by my own master as a teacher of the lineage of the Mo-Pai.

In each generation of the Mo-Pai, only one student has managed to go beyond Level Three and complete Level Four and those above it—only one student in each generation, throughout a 2,400-year history, which gave me every reason to suspect that a certain middle-aged Greek had a snowball's chance in hell of making it. If that were the case, wouldn't circumstances have allowed it while I was a younger man?

VOICES FROM THE PAST

I have led a tumultuous life. My parents were Greek immigrants to the United States who had moved back to Greece when I was twelve. Going from metropolitan New England in 1971 to a small village in northwestern Greece at a time when a corrupt dictator controlled the country and ignorance bloomed had not pleased me at all. Rebellious by nature, I set off for the United States again by myself at the age of seventeen. Having renounced Greek culture, I sought out a replacement and became enamored of the East.

I had begun learning martial arts at the age of ten at a local YMCA in the States and continued—albeit with a disreputable teacher—in Greece when we moved to that country. The *junta* in Greece had done its best to suppress information and culture, but, unknowingly, they had allowed one very significant television show to slip through their censorship. That show was *Kung Fu* with David Carradine (for younger readers, I am referring to the original series), and it changed my life. When I moved back to the States, the martial arts became both my anchor and my helm as I tried to make my way in a society I only partially understood and to which I was, at best, the scion of cheap labor.

During this time, having the ability to make my own rules meant that I had no umbilicus—I felt at home all over the world, having traveled much and been exposed to many diverse cultures. On the other hand, I was constantly insecure for the simple reason that I questioned everything, took nothing at face value, and rejected what roots I had been born with.

When a man wants to make a bonsai, he first seeks out the proper sapling to twist to his designs. I have a feeling that God follows the same modus operandi. I was that bonsai sapling, and every so often the Gardener snipped a leaf, or added another turn to a wire.

I decided to settle in Greece in 1992. At the time, I thought my reasons for doing so were personal, but this decision instigated a whole series of "coincidences" that led to me becoming John Chang's student and, as a result, pursuing a specific path from which I could no longer withdraw. By choosing to live in the Balkans during the time when conflicts in Bosnia and Kosovo, the Albanian civil insurrection, and constant tensions with Turkey were a daily reality, I was allowed to see how truly ephemeral life is. The streets of Athens were filled with the maimed begging for coins. It was a sight I had become accustomed to in the Orient, but not one I had ever expected to see in the West.

Most modern Greeks found shelter from that reality by becoming overly materialistic and hedonistic. (Everybody was sleeping with everybody else; there were a score of TV shows satirizing the fact.) I, however, saw things differently. I sought solace by becoming more devoted to the spiritual, trying to follow my own destiny and immersing myself in my master's training.

Standing on my mountaintop, screaming up at heaven, I remembered the one startling realization that had brought me to that hermitage. It was still warm that fall, and I would have preferred to be lying on a beach on a Greek island rather than being where I was. But the sudden insight had swept over me and had stripped me of any choice in the matter. Like a thunderbolt in the midst of the night, it had hit me, and I woke sweating, twisting and turning: *the forgotten side of ourselves.*

I slipped quietly from the bed but saw that I had already awakened Doris. In the dark I padded from the bedroom to the living room of our modest apartment.

She found me sitting quietly, drinking my village moonshine and smoking a cheap Cuban cigar. It was three in the morning. I had not turned on the lights.

"What's wrong?" she asked.

"The forgotten side of ourselves. It's been taken from us."

Doris sat down next to me. "This had better be worth waking me up in the middle of the night," she said.

That evening we had seen the award-winning film *The Sixth Sense,* about a little boy with enough natural extrasensory perception to see the spirits of the dead, and the problems this ability causes him in daily life. In a society that no longer believes in such things, the boy routinely questions his sanity, unwilling to accept what he is experiencing. But perhaps he isn't at all insane. Perhaps his experience is much more common than we think. I said as much to Doris.

"Are you saying that everyone has experiences of this sort, but is unwilling to talk about them for fear of being ridiculed?" she asked.

"No, I think that most people's experiences are for the most part figments of their imagination. But some are true—let's say that about 2 percent are real."

"And . . .?"

"What's the most important of my master's powers?"

"Are you saying that it's his ability to talk to spirits?"

"That little boy in the movie has what the Chinese call yin eyes. He can see and talk to the spirits of the dead. He is a shaman."

She waited quietly. I stood and began to pace in the darkness. The cigar went out—I didn't really smoke, anyway, but somehow it had suited the dramatic intimations of my revelation.

"In Neolithic times every village had its shaman. He spoke to the spirits of those who had recently departed, and helped them make the transition. Just like that little boy in the movie."

She grasped it then. I saw it shake her, and she nodded.

"Yes," I said. "We still need the shaman to survive as a species. Just like a newborn baby needs to be raised by its parents—it can't survive by itself, right?—a newly deceased human needs a shaman to help make the transition to another state of being."

I bowed my head. "They took them away from us, Doris. They took them away so that they could better control us. The shaman was replaced by the priest, and spirituality by dogma."

One of the main lessons that I learned from John Chang was that all things in the Universe are natural; there is no such thing as the supernatural, nor can one in truth speak of metaphysics. Everything on this planet—including ghosts, goblins, and elves, should they exist—is as natural as the stock market and beaver dams. Twice I have seen my master discuss sports with the dead, and they answered his questions matter-of-factly.

There are three institutions that seem to have developed together in human history: warfare, empire, and organized religion. It was not until ten thousand years ago that warfare, for instance, became an intrinsic part of our lives. It followed swiftly on the heels of systematized agriculture and larger settlements. Before that time, people had lived together in peace, for the most part, and violence between men was sporadic. The Norwegian explorer Fridtjof Nansen, who in 1888 made a historic journey across the ice fields of Greenland, encountered the last Eskimos there to live the same way that their forefathers had, in total harmony with the harsh land that bore them.

The Eskimos had shamans to guide them and teach them how to live in accord with the will of heaven.

Being able to speak with the spirits of the dead and have the society you live in accept that ability at face value means that people understand the laws of consequence. John Chang had spoken to me repeatedly about karma and the Fields of Retribution or Reward that the spirit enters into immediately after death. You must pay what you owe or receive what is owed to you before you can move on to whatever follows. This is something that the ancient shamans understood and passed on to those around them. People accepted what these men and women told them for the simple reason that their knowledge had been shown to be true.

For those who would scoff, let me say that this same methodology applies today to all people in all kinds of circumstances. The average housewife does not understand the electronics inside her microwave oven or the principles of physics that allow such a device to perform. Nevertheless, this does not prevent her from making use of the appliance. Human society has always been like this; it is the direction and the sum of our knowledge that has changed over the millennia, not the methodology of belief. The shaman differed from the priest in that the shaman himself had to display specific abilities rather than merely represent a given dogma that an organized religion had passed on as truth. The shaman had to have power—he was trained and tested by others like himself and had to prove himself routinely to those around him. People were more immediately concerned with survival in those days and did not have the luxury of wasting their efforts. Nor was the life of a true shaman any great joy; he acted out of duty to his fellow man and to the Divine Breath that inspires all.

When society became a prize to be won and controlled by those who would have power over other men, the shamans were the first to go because they represented the greatest threat. Those who would be kings removed the shamans, possibly by killing large groups of them, and replaced them with a priesthood (understanding that people will always have a need to approach the Divine). This strategy has been used many times throughout the history of mankind.

One such case in point that strikes home to me, more so because I am named after Constantine, is the establishment of Christianity as a state religion by the Roman emperor and saint Constantine the Great. Though this example occurs millennia after the deliberate extermination of the shamans I referred to, it is accurately recorded in historic annals and can be readily researched. Because most Western nations are Christian today, it will perhaps serve as the best example to get the message across.

The cosmopolitan nature of the Roman Empire in the first three centuries of this millennium meant that there was a philosopher or preacher lurking in every corner, promoting new and unfamiliar ideas. To the Greek in their city-states, precursors to the Romans, the presentation of new religious concepts was considered so dangerous that the philosopher Socrates had been put to death and the philosopher Anaxagoras had been jailed for the charge of introducing new doctrines. The international nature of the Roman Empire along with its cultural diversity, however, made such exclusion not only impossible but undesirable. From the time of Paul the Apostle, various cults based on Christ's teachings had spread around the Mediterranean and had grown disputatious. With new ideas spreading throughout the ranks, each local bishop promoted his own opinions and fought to see them accepted.

Christianity had, by the end of the first century, become a significant social force in spite of Roman efforts to stop it. However, at the same time, the doctrinal gulf between groups calling themselves Christian had grown too great to be ignored. Over the next few centuries various creeds prospered based on the writings and opinions of local bishops such as Justin of Samaria, Irenaeus of Asia Minor and Lyons, Marcion of Sinope, Tertullian of Carthage, Cyprian of Carthage, Clement of Alexandria, Montanus of Asia Minor, and Arius of Alexandria, to name a few. Also during this time, an eccentric group of Christians in the Near East became involved with Jewish mysticism and evolved into a group believing the theology known as Gnosticism (from the Greek word *gnosis*, or "knowledge"). It was a doctrine that accepted Jesus as a divine teacher, but rejected outright the dogmas of the Resurrection, apostolic tradition, and the mission of Jesus as taught by mainstream Christianity. According to Gnosticism, the God of the Old Testament was the source of all misery in life. To make matters worse, those who espoused this belief system claimed that they possessed a secret oral tradition from Jesus himself, and rejected the authority of all local bishops outright. Gnosticism took hold rapidly in Egypt, and began spreading to the other Roman provinces.

By the dawn of the fourth century, then, Christianity was widespread throughout the Mediterranean basin, but with no one creed or canon to unify its members. And so we arrive to Constantine and his edicts.

In 313, Emperor Constantine sent to his local governors a series of elaborate letters in which it was said that "complete toleration" should be extended to anyone following the teachings of Christ (in whatever shape and form, for the moment)—or any other cult, for that matter. The Edict of Milan, as this series of letters was called, had the effect of legalizing Christianity throughout the Roman Empire.

Historians have debated why the Edict of Milan was issued in the first place. To me it seems quite obvious: It was due to the growing political power of Christians of diverse dogma, and the strategic decision made by Constantine to use a single religion as a unifying factor for his multiethnic state. The Romans had the example of Alexander the Great to guide them and knew that, if the Empire was to last, cultural integrity was a necessity. The emperor understood well that the Christians were becoming so numerous as to represent a considerable political force should they ever become organized under one banner. He opted to make that banner his, and followed a policy of intimidation the likes of which Stalin himself would be proud.

Constantine was born in what is Serbia today and was quite familiar with the breadth of the Roman Empire of his day. He knew the Balkans and Asia Minor well. I am of the opinion that he planned on moving his capital from Rome to the East for decades for reasons of personal security, and that he used Christianity as the means to accomplish his goal. What better way to assimilate diverse ethnic groups than by revising their cultural identity through religion (or any other particular cultural marker)? Though he was in fact baptized a Christian before he died and was canonized after his death, I doubt the emperor had developed during his life the inner peace that sainthood implies—his canonization was assuredly a political decision.

Constantine was a practitioner of several religions even after his conversion to Christianity. His personal devotions were offered to Mars and increasingly to Apollo, revered as Sol Invictus, the "Unconquered Sun"; indeed it seems Constantine presented Christ as Apollo (or vice versa) in later years.

The emperor was subjective and capricious. He sent prisoners of war to the lions; committed wholesale acts of genocide in his campaigns in North Africa; and was known for his arrogant, egotistical, and ruthless behavior—hardly what we have come to expect from a Christian saint. Despite his professed affection for the teachings of Christ, he had no qualms about executing his son Crispus for involving himself with his stepmother Fausta (and indeed it seems the stepmother in question was all for the liaison, since she got the axe within a year herself even though she had borne Constantine three sons).

The most significant event in Constantine's religious-political development occurred in 312, a year before the Edict of Milan, when he fought the Battle of Milvian Bridge against a rival claimant to the emperor's throne. Among his soldiers were many Christians following diverse doctrines. The scholar Lactantius, who was close to the imperial family, reports that during the night before the battle Constantine was commanded in a dream to place the sign of Christ on the shields of his soldiers. Twenty-five years later Eusebius gives us a more elaborate and quite different account in his *Life of Constantine*: While Constantine and his army were on their way to Rome, Eusebius claims, they observed a strange phenomenon in the sky in broad daylight. A cross of light and the words "by this sign you will be victor" (*hoc signo victor eris*) appeared to them. It was during the next night that Christ appeared to Constantine and instructed him to place the heavenly sign on the battle standards of his army. Unfortunately, at least six different versions of the story have survived from different people who claimed to have heard it from the emperor himself, so we will never truly know what happened. As a monument to his victory at Milvian, years later, Constantine raised a triumphal arch in Rome, which survives to this day. It bears testimony to Sol Invictus with reference to Christ "driving his chariot across the sky." Ultimately, Constantine commanded Christians to hold their services on Sunday, the day of the Sun. There can be no clearer tautology of Christ with Apollo.

Constantine became the sole Roman emperor in 324 and subsequently moved his capital to the former Greek city of Byzantium, renaming it Constantinople. He convened the First Ecumenical Council of the Christian Church the following year, during which his commandment to the bishops was simple: Come up with a consistent doctrine that is universal—or catholic—in nature, and quit all the squabbling among yourselves. The opening session was held on May 20, 325 in the great hall of the palace at Nicaea, with Constantine himself presiding and giving the opening speech. The council, after much deliberation, formulated a canon, which, although it was revised at the Council of Constantinople in 381–82, has become known as the Nicene Creed. A major role at the council was played by Athanasius, bishop of Alexandria. Arius, by the way, was condemned, as were the Gnostics.

Despite the very real danger of imperial wrath, however, the disputes continued, and Constantine himself wavered again and again. Eusebius of Nicomedia, a supporter of Arius and exiled in 325, was recalled in 327 and was soon established as the emperor's chief spiritual advisor. In 335, Athanasius, stubbornly unbending toward some of Constantine's policies, was sent into exile, was recalled, and was exiled again. So much for loyalty and the consistency of spiritual doctrine.

In short, it was imperial politics and the wealth of the Roman church, divvied up among those smaller congregations that followed the party line, more than theology itself, that finally governed the form Christian doctrine was to take. In due course, the Council of Nicaea became a permanent affair, designed to stamp out contrary opinions and create a formal, universal church organization structured in a manner similar to the political configuration of the Roman Empire itself.

Why was Christianity the vehicle of choice, you ask? It was perfect for the job. As an imported creed with countless interpretations, it could be re-engineered at will to suit imperial design. It was apocalyptic and messianic in nature, with salvation centering on the blessings of the Christ rather than on individual effort. Because the emperor and Church leaders were the formal representatives of Christ, it was up to them to bestow salvation on the deserving. In short, temporal and spiritual authority were rolled together seamlessly in a faith that was multiethnic in nature and open to all. What could be better? There are exponents who view these factors in a positive light, citing such theocracy as the unifying factor that empowered both the early Church and the Eastern Roman Empire, but I myself would hesitate to be so upbeat about it. Constantine and his successors made it policy to stamp out the old religion, forbidding worship of the ancient gods on pain of death and tearing down shrines or converting them by force to Christian churches. Thousands were cast into the flames as heretics or were exiled, their property forfeited and absorbed by the imperial treasury. Greek religion and philosophy, which focused on the worship of natural forces and the psychophysical development of the individual, were specifically targeted as posing the greatest threat, and barbarian leaders were encouraged to attack and destroy pagan strongholds when imperial armies could not.

Rather than elaborate further on the subject here, I would suggest that you browse through recorded history, where you will find many examples of purges of this sort. The annals of organized religion and empire are one and the same; indeed, in many instances organized religion was used to justify slavery!

The incredible truth discovered in making such a study is the consistent existence of an organized priesthood throughout the millennia in all the empires of man. The founders of most of today's great religions—Christ, Buddha, Mohammed—were all figures who, in essence, had spoken out against the organized clergy of their respective times and places. And yet an organized priesthood seemed to appear in every religion, sometimes despite the founder's fervent wishes to the contrary. Who is to say, then, what occurred before mankind took to writing down its past? Could a pogrom of those men and women connected to the world of the spirits have been instrumental in changing the shape of our society millennia in the past? In those very early times could the shamans integral to the human species, those very necessary individuals who could speak to the spirits of our dead, have been exterminated to make it easier for those who sought temporal authority to rule?

They have done away with the forgotten side of ourselves. I cried that night, shaken by the revelation. For a given number of people, evolution had decreed that a shaman was needed, an individual who could communicate with the shades of the dead, who could see the strands of karma. That person could speak to the spirits of those who had passed on, and, in doing so, aid both them and the family and friends they had left behind. I had seen it repeatedly in the Mo-Pai—when John communicated with a spirit and his students and friends gathered around him, it was the most natural thing in the world. It made the terror of death fade before the realization that our consciousness did, indeed, verifiably pass on to another shape and form. Death was simply a transition, not the end. But the institution of a priesthood in essence means that a secular authority decides who will be the intermediary between man and the Divine, rather than allowing the will of heaven and the force of evolution to decide this on their own.

"Our power is a *natural* power," my Master told me one day during training. "It is the force of nature within ourselves. Trust in nature to teach you the principles of the Universe." But we as a species have done away with nature. Supreme in our arrogance, we pretend to have surpassed her mysteries. She is of no use to us.

In his vanity and ignorance mortal man has set himself above God. The last ten thousand years have been a mere heartbeat in the chronicles of evolution, a split second in the timeless eyes of heaven. The effects of our loss are not yet firmly established; there is still time to turn things around. Yet many great teachers of the past have tried to do just that and failed, not the least of whom was Mo Tzu, the founder of the lineage headed in this generation by my own master, John Chang. (Please see appendix 1, note 2.)

Which brings us back to my mountaintop. I was at a loss for what to do with the knowledge I had been blessed with. How could I hope to succeed where men who had been truly remarkable had faltered? I was no shaman. I was not a *hsien*, an immortal, like John Chang. I wasn't even that great a martial artist or scientist. I was Mr. Mediocre, the Jack-of-All-Trades, the average man; I could do all things but excelled at none.

Yet I was willing. God, was I willing. I would fight as hard as was necessary to have the truth put forth once again. *Timeo Danaos et dona ferentis,* Virgil had written in his *Aeneid*—"Fear the Greeks even when they are bearing gifts." I would use my wiles against the system by turning their own weapons against them, beginning with hard science. I knew that the yin field, that dark energy of chaos that coexists with our space-time, would be a difficult thing to prove to the scientific community. But I reckoned that if my master was willing, I could confirm to the world at large that we have a very distinct and specific dynamism that courses through our bodies and fuels our life force—the force of the yang ch'i, solar fire.

The difficult part would be getting John to cooperate. I had set up meetings three times with noted scientific authorities—once with a Harvard professor and twice with a Nobel Prize-winning physicist.[5] In the first case, John had been distrustful; the Harvard professor's association with powerful financial lobbies had given him cold feet. In the latter case, he had actually been willing to meet and work with the man, but the insurrection that had erupted in Indonesia had thrown a wrench into the works not once but half a dozen times. Getting everybody going in the same direction would be nearly impossible, but it was something that I was obsessed with by that point.

Computer simulation of the behavior of a system of binary opposites, using fractal mathematics, had resulted in depictions that resembled our Universe. As such, once I had experimental data, the math would be simple; I knew I could prove yin and yang to the world. In fact, the conversation I had with the Nobel-laureate physicist ran something like this:

"But surely this [yin and yang] is just poetry, or at best an illustration of the ideals of personal conduct," he said.

"No, we are discussing actual physical forces. Niehls Bohr . . ."

"Yes, *contraria sunt complementa*, but he was talking about an approach to learning, not a revision of physics."[6]

---

5. John was sworn by his own master never to demonstrate before nonstudents, but I had arranged circumstances to be in accord with his oath. I will not go into the details here.

6. The physicist Sir Niehls Bohr, after visiting China, had chosen the yin-yang symbol as his coat of arms, complete with the epigraph *contraria sunt complementa* (opposites are complementary). The symbol and phrase still mark his gravestone.

"Are you sure, professor? I think that he had seen something that shook him when he visited China, something that he spent his whole life looking for afterward but could not find. And Poincaré never really gave up looking for the ether."

"Young man," he said, sipping his tea," I can see that you are sincere and dedicated. If you are right, it will change everything. . . ." He paused, not for effect but to let me know that he had grasped the ramifications, all the way to the end, in the brief span of our discussion. "Everything as we know it. But I myself think that you have been simply duped by the Chinese."

Time would tell. The concepts, however, were so intriguing and fundamental that people would be willing to listen. One man could do only so much, in any case; I was amenable to sitting back in my rocking chair and enjoying the blaze if I could just manage to light the fire.

I would begin with the yang and leave the rest up to the will of heaven.

Filled with resolve, I stopped screaming up at the clear evening sky. Perhaps the Deity had heard my cries and, for a time, calmed the anger in this little pest's soul. I walked over to where the ground dropped off and watched the sun set over the blue Aegean as an endless forest rolled down craggy cliffs beneath me to the sandy shore three thousand feet below. I filled my lungs with pine-scented air. It quickly became dark, as was usual on that peak, and a cold wind blew through the treetops. People avoided the place where I had chosen to stay, calling it haunted. In the month I lived there, my only visitors had been a few shepherds who stopped by to say hello but did not remain for long. I myself had no problems with the spirits who resided there—I knew them for what they were.

Wishing I had a beer, I strolled back down to the cabin. I still had to cook my dinner and put in two more hours of meditation before bidding good night to the owls and their quarry, the field mice that thrived on that wooded crest.

Chapter 2
METAL

Living up in the mountains was simple. I woke in the morning with the sun, relieved myself a few hundred yards away from the cabin, ate whatever was handy, and began training. I put in eight hours of training a day in retreat; the rest of the time I relaxed or went to look for food and water.

The shack was built on the ridgeline of a mountain peak. My student George had built it roughly a hundred feet from the very summit, in a small depression nearby. Surrounded by pine trees, the shack was fairly well shielded from the wind and rain and was invisible until you were almost on top of it. A devout Buddhist of the Tibetan Karma Kargyu lineage, George had wanted a place where he could meditate in solace and not be disturbed. He had been more than successful in his endeavor; I considered the building of this cabin a monument to human persistence. The site had been chosen by a Tibetan lama, who had told George plainly that it had great power. Lucky me to have had circumstance work so well in my favor.

The main danger faced by anyone residing at the cabin was lightning, for reasons obvious and not, as we will see. As I have mentioned, the locals were afraid of the place, not least of all for this lightning that continually fell on and around the peak.

"Aren't you afraid of staying up there all by yourself?" a shepherd's wife asked me during one of my daily sojourns to a nearby spring.

"No, not at all," I answered. "Should I be?"

"It's a . . . it's a frightening spot," she stammered, and I caught the wisp of thought uppermost in her mind. She wanted to say that the spot was cursed, that weird things were known to happen there.

"Why don't you go camp over on the other ridge, where the shepherds stay?" she continued. "You know, we've built three churches up there to protect us."

"It's quite all right," I told her quietly. "They won't bother me; I've made friends with them."

Her eyes widened and I could see that she knew who and what I was talking about. She mumbled something and beat a hasty retreat, behind her back making the sign against the evil eye.

It was around noon, during the second week that I was up there, that life managed to surprise me once again, despite all my experiences with John Chang. It was a hot day, and I distinctly remember snoring with pleasure on the floor of the shack, lazily catching up on my sleep after a large meal of boiled rice and eggs. Fat black flies were buzzing around the mosquito netting, but I slept contentedly, knowing that they could not disturb me. The previous evening, the owls and foxes chasing mice, rabbits, and each other had kept me awake—people do not appreciate how noisy nature can be at night. The cabin, with whatever meager supplies of food I had stored on wires around it, attracted rodents, who in turn attracted predators. Some nights the racket was incredible.

The explosion shocked me out of deep sleep. I grabbed the Nepalese *kukri*[1] that was my main tool and only weapon and rolled out of the cabin, hitting the ground hard and cursing myself for not being more paranoid.

The mountains of Greece were no longer completely safe. Armed bands of Albanians routinely made their way through the wilds, trying to get to the major cities in search of work. Normally they left people alone, but there had been many cases of armed robbery. I did not condemn them; these were desperate people whose lives and

---

1. A compact, inwardly curving short sword.

country the circumstances of politics had destroyed. But neither did I go looking for trouble. Things had grown progressively worse in recent years, with the wars in Kosovo and Bosnia and the abundance of illegal firearms to be found on the black market. There were all sorts of paramilitary wackos on maneuvers in the mountains, of Eastern European extraction for the most part and of every political conviction. In short, it was good to give armed bands a wide berth.

A second explosion rocked the silence and I relaxed even as I was running toward the ridgeline. It had been too loud for a grenade, and it was too far off to immediately concern me, probably at the base of the ridge.

I looked over the promontory and was stunned to see bulldozers and cranes below me. The explosions had been dynamite charges.

What the . . .?

I worked my way down the mountain path an hour or so later. One of the shepherds I knew told me that a mining company had bought half the mountain for a pittance, it seemed. They were strip mining for gold and nickel, something I thought was illegal in the European Union. Equally exasperating was my recollection that the whole area was supposed to be national forestland and my subsequent realization that some politician and his cronies had obviously been paid off. I had heard Greece called the Bananaless Republic, in honor of the corruption evident in the public sector.[2] Before me stood living proof, for the umpteenth time, that the appellation was warranted.

Short of attacking the mining site and decapitating the workers (which was a *very* tempting thought), there was nothing I could do. Cursing human greed with every step, I made my way up the trail back to the shack. One more patch of pristine wilderness was about to be destroyed. The chemicals used by the miners would consume everything in a few short years, of that I was sure.

---

2. The visible dishonesty and prohibitive cronyism manifest in Greece are incomprehensible to the average Westerner. It is only recently that I have come to understand that they are a survival trait left over from 2,100 years of slavery.

For the next week I could time a clock by the dynamite charges, which went off precisely at twelve and two every day. I made sure to be doing chores during that time, so that the mining would not disturb my meditations. I could hear the bulldozers and compressors at work during the daylight hours, but their sounds were too far off to bother me. It was ironic; I had come to the wilderness to escape the sounds of man and his cities, but industry had followed at my heels.

Wonderful.

CHILDREN OF THE INNER EARTH

It was in the dreams of sleep that they first approached me.

The night had been quiet; my trap of setting pieces of food about a hundred yards from the shack to lure away the mice and the owls with them had worked. I was smugly enjoying a good solid sleep when I saw the dream.

Now you must understand that by virtue of my training I am familiar with the process of lucid dreaming. As such, I can easily slip into a conscious state of mind when dreaming and, on a good day, can control my dreams for a fairly long time.

I saw myself sleeping in a dark place, and was aware that I felt safe and was welcome there. I sat up in my sleeping bag as two shadowy forms approached. They were neither hostile nor friendly. I saw that behind them there were many others trying to press forward but held back by the first two.

"*Man,*" a voice said inside my head. It was coming from the taller of the two shadows.

"Yes."

"*Do not fear us.*"

"I do not. Hello, *King of the Mountain.* It is you, isn't it?"

"*Yes. Greetings. It has been many years since we spoke with mortal man. Most who come here do not listen.*"

"*They shrink from your power.*"

"*?????*"

"Deep down inside they are afraid of you, no matter what they may think consciously."

"I don't understand."

"Never mind."

The King of the Mountain is an extremely powerful earth elemental. He lives near the very peak and has shaped for himself a stunningly human face in stone over the millennia. It was this face, and the bizarrely human features of the others of his kind around him, that drove visitors away from this place (figure 5).

Fig. 5. The King of the Mountain

I had seen others like him before in the Orient. In Japan his kind were revered as *kami-sama*, spirits of nature inherent to the land. I had studied Tendai Buddhism at a temple near Tokyo where both

Fig. 6. A spirit rock in Japan

the laity and priests had introduced me to one particular boulder, an elemental that had miraculously cured several people of terminal illnesses and, I was assured, had even saved the life of a child during an earthquake (figure 6).

All ancient cultures had names for these beings. In modern times they have been categorized as fixtures of superstitious nonsense or, at best, as the objects of quaint local cultural beliefs.

In my dream, then, I was speaking to a quaint local cultural belief. Perhaps he had simply been carved into the stone thousands of years ago by Neolithic man, and I was letting my imagination run wild. After all, it *was* a dream. Or perhaps it was real. In any case, I was enjoying it.

"Thank you for the incense you leave us every day."

"You're most welcome."

I then sensed hesitation on the part of the King of the Mountain.

"How can I help you?" It was obvious that they wanted something

from me, otherwise we would not be having this conversation. They did not like people, and for the most part remained quiet.

There was a long silence, and then the second shadowy figure spoke. I called her the queen, presumptuously, anthropomorphically, probably erroneously attributing a sex to her. She stood to the right and just below the king, though, and had the air of being second in command. For some reason I got a definite feminine vibe from her; maybe it was the long flowing gown she "wore."

"Pain," she said.

"Why?" I asked.

"They are eating away at the veins of power inside the earth."

And then I knew. I understood completely. The miners were killing them.

I did not question the fact that the distance from the peak to the miners was more than a mile—who knew what these beings were and how far their domain extended? Who knew what they required in order to exist? That they had been here for millennia, I had no doubt.

Mo Tzu, the founder of my master's lineage, had taught us 2,400 years ago that there were essentially three kinds of spirits in the world: the spirits of heaven, the spirits of the mountains and rivers, and the ghosts of men who have died.[3] Now, you must understand something about the ancient Chinese and archaic cultures in general—they were eminently practical and fighting was a routine part of their existence. In fact, they enjoyed combat, which is why they considered it an art form, something through which beauty may be expressed. A court system based on Judeo-Christian ethics did not hold sway and the average man could expect to kill several times in his life, if he himself were to survive. People who consider ancient beliefs as quaint or irrational are way off base—had these certitudes not been suitably pragmatic, they would have been dis-

---

3. Mo Tzu, Hsun Tzu, and Han Fei Tzu, *The Basic Writings of Mo Tzu, Hsun Tzu, and Han Fei Tzu*, ed. and trans. Burton Watson (New York: Columbia University Press, 1967).

posed of along with their proponents. Convictions of this sort were a survival trait, and shysters could expect to be put to death.[4] It is only since religion and empire began to walk hand in hand that practical knowledge has been subject to attack and ridicule, for obvious reasons.

It seemed that these temporary neighbors of mine were in real trouble.

"*I don't know that I can help you,*" I told the queen in my dream. "*There isn't really anything I can do.*"

"*Why are they doing this?*" she asked. "*We have not attacked them.*"

"*To them, you do not exist.*"

At this she seemed puzzled. "*But we are here! You men know we are here.*"

"*No. Only a few villagers know that now.*"

"*But . . .*"

"*Our lives are short. Like the animals of the forest, we are born, breed, and die in a heartbeat.*"

"*We have been forgotten.*"

"*Yes.*"

The beings remained quiet. They simply stood there.

"*I have to think about this for a while,*" I continued. "*I will see what I can do.*"

"*Yes, shaman,*" the king said. "*Thank you. You are welcome in this place.*"

And with that I was awake, shocked, sitting up in my sleeping bag inside the cabin, listening to the sounds of the night. My heart was beating incredibly slowly and I felt like I had been drugged. They had pulled my metabolism down to the lowest levels of brain activity so that they could speak to me. I was sluggish and tired; whatever had transpired had drained my body of yin energy.

What did you call me? I shouted out in my mind. *Shaman?! I am not!*

---

4. Which is not to say that everything they believed in was true. Even today, our science is a best guess toward the inner workings of the Universe. There are many weak areas in our knowledge and many things that we cannot explain. Knowledge is an *approximation*—how powerful we are depends on how close to reality that approximation is. It has always been this way, throughout the ages of man.

I could never be that. I was not born with the talent. Besides, I have degrees in two fields of engineering.

It was the evening of the new moon. I went outside to relieve myself, the sounds of the night surrounding me as I walked. On the way back, I looked up at the king's stone face looming over the cabin. He seemed to smile down at me.

THAT WHICH TRANSMUTES

So that the reader can better understand my conversation with the earth elementals, I am going to have to digress in length and explain further the philosophy behind the activities of yin and yang.

In *The Magus of Java*, I proposed a model explaining the phenomenon of ch'i that was essentially based on a millennia-old Chinese theory but also incorporated today's theories on space and time. Taoist teachings tell us that yin ch'i and yang ch'i are present in everything alive. John Chang had given me a spectacular demonstration of yin energy, using that force to absorb momentum and send it into "nowhere." John had passed yin ch'i into my body and fired an air rifle (which I had just used to shoot through a metal can) into my palm. Something had stopped the pellet so that I felt only the gentlest of touches. Moreover, the pellet had not been deformed in any way and there had been no generation of heat. Whatever had absorbed the momentum of the slug had done so without conserving its energy, something that is impossible according to today's physics. Later, John told me that he used gravity to accomplish this feat, and that gravity is one of the several intrinsic yin energies in our world. He had bound the force of gravity to his will in order to demonstrate this.

As a Level Two student of the Mo-Pai, I have worked with yang ch'i on a daily basis and have come to identify two characteristics intrinsic to its behavior. First of all, it is hot. John Chang uses it to perform pyrogenesis, setting crumpled newspapers on fire. At my level, it has scarred my palms near the acupuncture points of the pericardium meridian, the marks resembling something like the stigmata from the Catholic tradition. These stigmata are essentially localized hyperemia generated by the flow of bioenergy, which the doctors monitoring me could not explain with Western medicine (figure 7). I could use those "wounds" to feel the condition of a patient's body, sensing the flow of the ch'i throughout his or her organs and limbs.

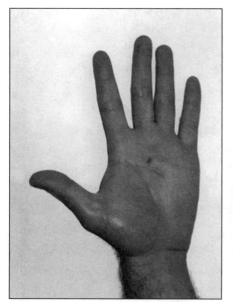 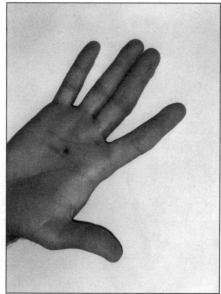

Fig. 7. The "stigmata" (localized hyperemia) generated by the flow of bioenergy. The phenomenon appears here on both the left and right hands.

The second characteristic of yang energy is that it wants to go *up*. I can feel it rising in my body whenever I have done my exercises—it does not want to settle in my dantien, but wants to go to the top of my head and burst out, if it could. From this simple sensation (coupled with the fact that I had seen John Chang levitate from the ground in defiance of natural law) I have come to understand something that Chinese sages have been saying for the last three thousand years: The yang energy exists in opposition to the yin.

And if gravity is a yin ch'i, what is the yang ch'i? The yang ch'i must be a force correlated to solar nuclear fusion, and this force that fuels the sun fuels our lives on earth as well. (Please see appendix 2.)

The Universe has proved itself many times to be fractal in nature. It is therefore logical to assume that a force existing macrocosmically would also exist microcosmically inside our own being. Our current science accepts the notion that were it not for the dynamism of nuclear fusion serving as an expansive force, our sun would collapse under the force of its own gravity. What this means is that all stars are battlefields between gravity and some force providing outward pressure, and that this battle shapes our space-time.

When most people think of gravity, they remember the basics learned in high school: One mass exerts an attractive force on another, and it is this attractive force that keeps us on the planet's surface. But let's take this truism one step further and define things more precisely: Gravity is that force in the Universe that wants all matter to collapse into a single mass, and ultimately into one singularity. That is to say, gravity is that force that seeks to compact space and time into a single, massive black hole. The intrinsic yin ch'i used by John Chang to achieve his spectacular, energy-absorbing demonstrations must be related to the force of gravity. It is this dynamism that absorbs energy and sends it into "nowhere."

Solar fire, on the other hand, is the expansive force that creates space and time and keeps it extant. Western science calls this solar force nuclear fusion. The ancient scholars of China called it yang ch'i. They are one and the same. Macrocosmically the combat between the two forces of yin and yang define the nature of reality. Microcosmically their interaction fuels our life force. (Isn't it logical to hypothesize that, should such a contest comprise the fundamental natural condition of our Universe, our own bodies and our very life force would reflect it?)

In *The Magus of Java*, I proposed the theory that John Chang's power, those energy blasts of his that feel like you are being zapped by a high-voltage electrical current, is attributable to nuclear fusion. I (and other scientists) have tried to measure this power with instruments, but no voltage or current was evident. And yet no one could deny the very real force of these blasts, which indeed could be used to perform work as defined by modern physics (for instance, causing a glass of water to boil or delivering tremendous momentum). So what was happening? John's power is either mechanical in nature or the result of a dynamism we could not pinpoint. Since no movement of electrons was evident, and since John's power can be transferred through metallic objects over long distances (making it clearly not mechanical), Occam's razor suggested to me that it was due to nuclear fusion. (In proposing this theory, however, I have made matters more complex than Occam would wish—I have suggested that this nuclear fusion is brought about by yang ch'i, a factor not recognized by current biophysical law.)

I will add, very briefly, primarily for those technocrats out there, that there is a case for assuming that John's "electricity" is radio frequency (RF) current. This type of electromagnetic wave is not readily measurable with conventional current and voltage meters, but rather requires a specialized oscilloscope. When we look at the electromagnetic spectrum as a whole, we find that two forms of emissions from the sun are able to penetrate to the surface of the earth undiminished: visible light and radio waves. Perhaps there is something inherent in RF emissions under natural law that allows their propagation throughout the human body.

Having said that, we still have to explain the power source that is generating these waves. In essence, we can interpret the entire electromagnetic spectrum as being a yang phenomenon. Even if a future study shows that the energy produced by John Chang is RF current, amazing as this is by itself, it will only lead to more questions as to how those waves are generated.

In the end I believe that we will uncover that my master's dantien does indeed act much like a star being orbited by a black hole, and that the primary energy source is attributable to nuclear fusion. Only when we embrace the precept of *what happens macrocosmically must occur microcosmically* will we come to understand the mystery of ch'i. I believe this, in turn, will lead to the unified field theory so dearly coveted by modern scientists.

There is one more thing I can state unequivocally through my experiences with John Chang: Both yin ch'i and yang ch'i behave as both particle and wave phenomena—indeed, it would be no stretch of the imagination to state boldly that *ch'i has mass.* The appellations given by ancient cultures around the world to the term *bioenergy* (ch'i, pneuma, rlung, ruach, spiritus, prana) all refer to a vaporlike phenomenon, and I have seen this to be true firsthand. Ch'i has mass much the same way that smoke has mass. When I first tested for the completion of Level Two (and failed dismally), my student Spiros was present and assured me he had seen "something like smoke" rising out of my palms. John confirmed that this was indeed yang ch'i. In any case, enough said on this matter . . . for the moment.

On a cosmic scale, we can graphically depict the interaction of yin and yang as follows:

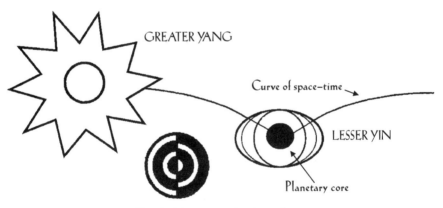

Fig. 8. Macrocosmic yin and yang

The t'ai chi symbol shown is the archaic form, which better represents the clash of the two forces, though not their transition with space and time.

You will notice that I labeled the center of the yin field as originating in the planetary core; there is a reason for this, one that will bring us back to our earth elementals before long. Imagine the yin

as the primal chaos that existed prior to our own Universe, a condition beyond space and time. This chaos is still very much a part of
our own reality, a sort of dark ether that opposes the light of the
stars, and yet is a prerequisite for our life force. The Taoist sages of
old and John Chang have taught us that everything alive must have
both the yin and yang energies coursing in parallel through their
bodies. A wooden table is simply yang and is therefore lifeless, while
a tree has both yin and yang. But if the yang ch'i comes from the sun,
then where does the yin ch'i come from?

We know much more about the earth's core than we used to.
We appreciate that metallic elements in high concentration are required somewhere in the interior of the earth to generate the planet's
evident magnetic field. We know that this metal must have fluid
properties at very high temperatures. While contemporary (1998)
estimates tell us that the earth's solid inner core (there is an outer
core as well) may be one single huge crystal of iron 2,400 km in
diameter, I will stick my neck out and agree with an earlier model
(1996), which predicts that the core has a dispersion of 4 percent
nickel as well. My reasoning for this is based on the functioning of the
keris, a short sword of the Malay Archipelago.

In *The Magus of Java*, I explained much of the magic of the keris, a
weapon made from meteorites of a specific nature. A talisman inserted
into the metallic body of the keris binds the maker's spirit to the
weapon, along with his solemn oath to protect the owner of the
short sword. A keris can be capable of flying through the air or boil-
ing water from a distance; I have seen some incredible demonstrations of power from an individual keris at John Chang's home.

In effect, this sword serves as an antenna to the maker's spirit.
When a keris is called upon, in essence the maker (*empu*) is called
upon to protect the owner of the sword. This practice may be
construed as sorcery, of that there can be little doubt, but whether
the magic is dark or white is left to the individual forger to decide.[5]

---

5. This type of process is not unique to the Malay Archipelago; I have seen similar talismans
from Tibet, India, and Polynesia, and one that is possibly from Arabia.

In the past, an empu consigned his spirit in such a manner as to protect the lineage and family of a man he cherished; I am sure that many such ghosts are less than happy when the talisman that binds them is bought and sold like jewelry.

The point is, the metallic body of the keris both contains and transmits the yin energy of the talisman for many centuries. A keris is composed of meteorite iron with a high nickel content, a trait that gives them their damascene appearance.

"Look at them! They think they can forge a keris from simple iron and nickel! They don't understand that a real keris must be forged from a meteorite!" John Chang had used these harsh words in private to me during a visit to a Javanese keris maker. We were watching a modern day empu toil away, forging pieces I myself thought were works of art.

"Why is that, Sifu?" I asked.

"Because only a meteorite can contain the yin energy of the talisman. Any keris that truly has power has been forged from a stone that has fallen from the sky," he answered.

It was upon hearing those words and remembering what I had learned of yin and yang that I understood that these meteorites were the heart of a planet that had once existed, but had been destroyed. They were pieces of its planetary core. Our earth's core, too, has a composition similar to the metal of the keris, and is both an antenna and transistor for yin energy. Somehow the core of our planet is in constant communion with the primal chaos, delivering the yin energy to us so that life may exist.

Several researchers have proposed the theory that the planet earth is one single living organism of which we as a species are a part.[6] It would be wonderful if this were true, but what is certain is that we need the yin energy from the core of the earth in order to survive. This energy is easily transmitted through the planet's mantle, but in order that it may be evenly distributed through the surface, a net-

---

6. Professors Lynn Margulis and James Lovelock among others. I am referring to the Gaia theory.

work comparable to the system of arteries and capillaries that feed the cells of our bodies with blood is required. This network is made up of the veins of metal ore that run through the crust, lodes that we as a species have been scavenging for the last four thousand years.

Before I go on, let me once again defend myself from those who would scoff. I doubt that anyone would dare argue in our age against the fact that the world is fractal in nature, self-replicating in form so that function may be attained. Coastlines are fractal, as is the beating of our heart. This is a fact that ancient cultures understood well. For example, two thousand years ago, through their meditations, Buddhists came up with the concept of *mandalas*, two dimensional fractal representations of a given aspect of our three-dimensional reality. Our bodies, too, are self-replicating microcosms of the Universe; there is no way around this.

Let's continue by looking at our biochemistry and the importance of metal to our life force. Everyone today knows that iron is a crucial component of our blood. As a basic constituent of hemoglobin, it is in fact iron that allows us to breathe.[7] Though iron makes up less than 0.004 percent of our body weight, without it we die. Much also has been written about the importance of minerals and electrolytes in our bloodstream—all, for the most part, metallic compounds. Once we understand how important metals are to the functioning of our bodies, can we disregard the conclusion that they may be crucial to the functioning of our planet as a whole?

The English word *metal* comes from the Greek word μέτάλλόν, which means "that which transmutes."[8] The word in itself should raise a few eyebrows, but since alchemy is a forbidden topic in our day and age, and since few people realize the source of the word, its meaning is ignored. Our modern physics insists that materials do

7. Hemoglobin is a protein containing four very long amino acid chains per molecule. Each chain is attached to a chemical structure we call a *heme group*, a ringlike organic compound to which in turn one iron atom is attached. Each molecule of hemoglobin, then, contains four iron atoms, and it is to these iron atoms that oxygen bonds reversibly, allowing our cells to breathe.

8. From the verb μέτάλλάσσώ to transmute.

not transmute of their own accord. Cold fusion is impossible, biological fusion preposterous. One could lose his place in academia for suggesting such a thing. Hush.

And yet it is metal that again instigates one of the most perplexing controversies in Western medical theory. Several researchers[9] have suggested that electrically induced nuclear fusion (i.e., cold nuclear fusion) takes place inside the body all the time. Living cells have a potential difference across the cell wall that is due to the differential concentration of sodium ions (Na^+) and potassium ions (K^+) inside and outside the cell; this differential is called the transmembrane potential. The mainstream theory (called the *sodium-potassium pump*) proposes a mechanism to explain this potential whereby sodium is mechanically exchanged for potassium inside and outside the cell membrane. However, the logistics behind this model are complex and have never been proved. Proponents of the biological cold nuclear fusion theory, on the other hand, suggest that sodium, in the presence of oxygen, is nuclearly transmuted to potassium inside the cell (by biological cold fusion), and that the process should rightfully be labeled the *sodium-potassium transmutation*.[10] The potassium in this model is regarded as a waste product, not an initiator of the reaction. Since excess potassium in the bloodstream is a deadly poison, treating it as a waste product on the cellular level, useful only in specific ratio to sodium to maintain a potential difference across the cell membrane, makes good sense.[11] Remember, the Universe follows this rule: *What occurs macrocosmically occurs microcosmically.* This rule applies on every scale in our fractal cosmos.

It may be, then, that life itself is animated by the transmutation of one metal to another. Perhaps the ancient Greeks knew what they were talking about when they labeled these elements "those which

---

9. L.C. Kervran, H. Komiki, H. Hillman, P.T. Pappas, S. Goldfein, and others.

10. Panos T. Pappas, *Electrically Induced Nuclear Fusion*, www.papimi.gr.

11. Hyperkalemia, excess potassium in the bloodstream, causes instant cardiac arrest and is thus usually fatal. The body does everything it can to keep the ratio of Na^+/K^+ constant, disposing of excess potassium in the urine.

transmute." Perhaps they realized how important metal is, and what its role is in the scheme of things.

So we have seen then that metal ions are supremely important for our life force both chemically (the iron in hemoglobin) and "alchemically" (the Na^+/K^+ exchange). And would metal be any less important to the life force of the planet as a whole? I am convinced that the metal crystal in the earth's inner core has very special properties that tie the planet to the yin field of the primal chaos. I am convinced that the network of veins of metallic ore in the earth's crust are there so that this yin energy may reach up to and be distributed through the planet's surface.

Metal is, in other words, a connecting element between the yin and the yang fields of existence. I believe that this is so because metal has properties in the electric, magnetic, solar bioenergetic (yang), and yin fields.

Which finally brings us back to our earth elementals and my lucid dreaming. My master has told me repeatedly: Everything on the earth is yang, but the earth itself is yin. We ourselves are yang creatures and have little metal in our bodies by weight (even though this metal is crucial). Is it so crazy to assume that entities could exist on (or in) the planet that make greater use of metal and its properties?

Lung Hu Shan, the Taoist monastery that was home to my master's teacher, Grandmaster Liao, is located in China's Jiangxi province, and Jiangxi is unusually rich in mineral resources. The area boasts the largest copper mine in Asia. Among the one hundred fifty minerals discovered in the world, Jiangxi has more than one hundred forty, and many of the veins of ore pass right under Lung Hu Shan. Extensive reserves of eighty-nine types of metallic ore have been discovered and thirty-three are among the top five in volume and quality in Asia. I am convinced that this is hardly coincidental, and it would be a significant step to prove someday that modern technology and ancient spirituality do indeed share a connection to the inherent power of metal.

The earth contains at least 40 percent metal by weight. The earth elementals are tied to metal to feed their life force, which is much more yin than yang. Ancient cultures around the world, which lived closer to nature and stumbled onto these beings frequently, referred to them as spirits or gods. Since the elementals are more yin than yang, such a distinction made sense. Perhaps they are indeed spirits.

The connection between yin, the earth, and the spirit world is as old as humankind. The rationale of Stone Age man holding his ceremonies in caves was simple: He wanted better access to the yin field so that he could more easily invoke those spirits he desired to communicate with. Anthropologists have found ritual offerings a mile under the earth in the cave of Tuc D'Audoubert, dating to approximately 13,000 B.C.E. The celebrated oracle of Acheron in my own country, where men sought out the shades of their ancestors in archaic times, is little more than a pit in the ground, but the whole area has an incredible amount of yin energy because of the nearby river.

There is another cave in Greece that better exemplifies the importance of yin and the role of caves in spiritual disciplines throughout the ages. It is located in Crete, on the peninsula of Akrotiri near Hania. There are two Greek Orthodox monasteries situated around this cave: an older, deserted one close to the seashore (Moni Katholikou, built in the sixth century C.E. and abandoned centuries later due to pirate raids), and a newer one higher up on the hillside (Moni Gouvernetou, built in the twelfth century by monks of the earlier monastery who wanted a more defendable location).

Three hundred yards down a steep path from Moni Gouvernetou is a large cave inside of which is built a small church. The true depth of the cave is unknown, since most of it has yet to be charted in our generation. One striking thing about it, though, is the large stalactite in its entrance chamber, which has the unmistakable shape of a bear. Perhaps even more interesting is that archaeological excavations have shown that the cave has a religious history.

Neolithic man worshiped the earth bear and the Mother Goddess there. In Minoan Crete, circa the seventeenth century B.C.E., the cave became a temple to Diktynna, a virgin Cretan goddess whose totem was the bear. She was followed by her classical Greek counterpart Artemis, another virgin deity to whom the bear was sacred, and who in Roman times became Diana. When the Greeks eventually

Fig. 9. The "earth bear" in the cave at Moni Gouvernetou, seen from both the side and the front

converted to Christianity (between the fourth and sixth centuries C.E.), the cave became a temple to the Virgin Mary of the Bears (Panagia Arkoudiotissa), and a baptismal font was built onto the stalactite, fed by the steady drip of a small spring. Hence the goddess worshipped in the cave changed her name, but not her essence, throughout the millennia. Today, fears of a pagan revival have caused the Greek Orthodox Church to "neglect" the small church and baptismal font, calling it idolatrous (figure 9). But tourists (mostly German) flock there by the thousands during the summer.

I, ever interested in traveling to such sites, felt the incredible yin energy in the cave when I visited there, and I understood the secret of its sanctity. I sought the inner recesses of its entrance chamber and sat down in meditation for hours, undisturbed until three young German girls, neopagans and devotees of Artemis, stripped and began to cavort naked in the font, splashing each other and laughing.

They were quite shapely, and while they did not see my shadowy figure sitting quietly in the alcove, it was difficult for me to ignore them. I was tempted to ask if they wanted company, but knowing well the fate of Actaeon, decided to remain quiet instead.[12]

Virgin goddesses aside, the point is that the yin energy, the earth, and the spirit world have always been tied together throughout our history. We should not, in our arrogance, dismiss the knowledge of primitive man as quaint superstition, for in doing so, we dismiss a major part of ourselves. We must never forget that those men and women are our ancestors, and that they chose to live the way they did for millennia. We should not erase for good the forgotten side of ourselves simply so that we may be better controlled by those who seek our servitude.

Addendum: Since initially writing these words I can smugly and happily report that the mining company, which planned on digging not fifty meters from where the king and queen lie, has been given the boot—at least for the time being. Yours truly began raving and frothing at the mouth in the Greek martial arts magazines. Local residents signed a petition as a result and the company had to cease operations. This having been said, the vein of the ore near the elementals is close to a thousand meters deep and represents a fortune to shareholders and, naturally, the politicians getting their piece. I do not know how long we can hold them off or what will happen to the earth elementals. They cannot leave their spot and go somewhere else.

---

12. Actaeon was a huntsman who was chasing a stag with his hounds when he came upon the goddess Artemis bathing in a spring. Enraged that a mortal man should see her in her nakedness, Artemis changed Actaeon into a stag and then set his own pack on him. The dogs tore him to pieces.

Chapter 3
MICROCOSM

I had come down from my mountaintop and rejoined society, a decision that generated no end of delight at first but frustrated me endlessly within a week. My initial problem was that talking was difficult, my vocal cords having become less used to doing so; I wondered what it was like to spend years in isolation, not having anyone to speak to and not being forced to converse with anyone. My master has spent years in the wild; he has mentioned to me that for the first six months he cried every day, but afterwards quickly lost the need and desire for society.

In any case, I had rejoined the rabid race that was urban Greece, delighting in the sights and sounds of civilization. We were sitting in a café in Glyfada, one of the southern suburbs of Athens. I had stumbled onto Spiro, my airline-pilot friend and student of *The Magus of Java* fame, who was convening with several of his flight-attendant friends on the suburb's trendy main strip.[1]

In order to make my blood pressure go up, Spiro skillfully (and maliciously, it seems) turned the conversation to bioenergy and spirituality. It turned out that everyone present had read some books and attended a few seminars, and, as a result, had abilities that made the

---

1. Liao Sifu, the noncorporeal grandmaster of the Mo-Pai, had caused a miniature rainstorm to pour down exclusively on my Volkswagon after I had broken an oath and told Spiro about my teacher during a long drive. The road around us remained dry.

powers of my own master pale by comparison. I nodded and mur-
mured my appreciation for a long time (with Spiro grinning gleefully as it went on) until I could no longer stand it and politely
interjected.

"Look," I said, "while I agree that powers of this sort exist, I
hardly think that they are common. I would guess that in order to
develop the abilities we are talking about, one needs to spend at
least twenty years in a monastery or hermitage somewhere, practicing meditation every day, and even then there's no guarantee."[2]

"How do *you* know?" one woman said hotly. In her previous
soliloquy she had just raised the dead with her healing touch and
had a lot to be defensive about.

"Well, it makes sense, doesn't it?" I replied. "You can't learn to
play tennis or the piano in one seminar—it takes years of practice,
right? You can' t get a Ph.D. by attending a lecture or a short course,
you have to go though elementary school first, then high school,
college, university, post-graduate work, all that good stuff. I'm sure
that things of a spiritual nature work like that as well—I mean,
everything that exists in the Universe is *natural* and should follow
the law of natural progression, right?"

They all nodded except for the woman who had just addressed
me. She continued her immoderate tone.

"Well," she scoffed, "that shows how much *you* know. Spiritual
power has to do with *initiation*, not practice. You get these gifts of
power from your teacher, not through working at them."

"I see. Would that it were so easy," I said. "Of course, this teacher
is paid handsomely for his gifts and his benevolence, right?"

In twenty-eight years of teaching, John Chang has not made one
dime from any of his students or patients; indeed, he is forbidden by
oath to do so. Not only that, but he routinely feeds us as well when we
visit, in appreciation of the money we spend on airfare and lodging.

---

2. It took John Chang eighteen years of dedicated effort to develop his powers following
daily instruction by Grandmaster Liao, a man who was at an incomprehensible level of
power himself.

She stood and put her hands on her hips, furious. "You shouldn't talk about things you know nothing about!" she huffed. "Who do you think you are, anyway?"

The girl later advised Spiro to be more judicious in choosing his friends.

WAVEFORMS

I myself have tried to be less obsessive in my studies with John Chang, and one method I've used with some success is to strive to uncover similar teachings within the course of human history. Truth, you see, is quite hard to come by and things are seldom as they appear to be—this is an axiom that we would all do well to heed. There is one rule, however, that seems to apply as far as discerning the ultimate reality of things: If separate efforts have yielded common results, chances are that the specific observation or conclusion is worth heeding. This is especially true if the individuals voicing these conclusions are isolated by five or six thousand miles and millennia of history and are members of mutually hostile ethnic groups. To get at the truth of things, then, you must be a detached and objective observer (something that is not easy), and try to uncover these common realizations.

By virtue of the way I grew up, I had few attachments. It was hard for me to be passionate about creed or country, for example—I was a true citizen of the world. Neither race nor creed made any difference to me; man was the same all over the globe, with identical passions, obsessions, and failings. As I grew older, I understood as well a truism that Somerset Maugham had written about long ago: Grandeur and pettiness reside side by side in the hearts of all men, and this is also often the case when applied to cultures as a whole.[3] But having such an outlook on life made it difficult to fit into any one place and even more difficult to understand people's fixation

---

3. W. Somerset Maugham, *The Moon and Sixpence*.

with things and theories that were intrinsic to their own belief system. It seemed that this perspective of mine was a freedom of sorts, but also a prison.

Let's take the Mo-Pai teachings on yin and yang, for example. It seemed that the concepts of yin and yang have been ubiquitous, their presence traceable far back in the mists of time. As I have said, the Mesopotamians had known them, as had the ancient Greeks, Indians, Persians, and Chinese. Like nearly all those who are familiar with it, at first I thought that the common yin-yang symbol defined the interaction of these two energies most precisely. It was not long, however, before I discovered that no human symbol could cover the entire scope of two primal forces of nature, as willing or inspired as the artist may be.

On the wall of a Chinese temple in Java, I found a thrilling depiction of yin and yang, one that immediately made me think of the chakras of Indian mysticism and the caduceus of the ancient Greek god Hermes (the Roman Mercury). Rather than the standard black and white circular image made popular by Western literature, this painting showed the two energies entwined like lovers, a male and female in form depicted with embracing serpentine coils. In a fluke of fate, I had run out of film at the time and was unable to take a photograph, but made a simple sketch instead (figure 10).

Fig. 10. The two energies of yin and yang entwined. From a Chinese temple in Java.

The caduceus, a symbol used by the ancient Greeks and today erroneously instituted as the emblem of medicine, shows two serpents entwined around a staff (figure 11a). The staff of Asclepius, the god of healing to the ancient Greeks, shows a single snake—that of the yin energy, I personally believe—coiled around the staff (figure 11b). A Mesopotamian vase in the Louvre, dating to 2000 B.C.E., once again

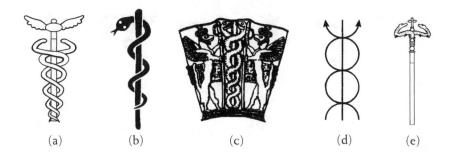

Fig. 11. caduceus (a); staff of Asclepius (b); Mesopotamian vase (c); standing wave (d); patriarchal staff (e)

shows the two coiled snakes (figure 11c); this is the oldest representation I myself have found. The astonishing fact to discover is that this symbol of the coiled serpent was eventually adopted by Christianity as well, becoming the standard carried even today by bishops and patriarchs of the Eastern Orthodox Church on their patriarchal staff.[4] (See figure 11e and 12.) Note that in figure 12, in the image on the right, the chakra called by the Hindus the "thousand-petalled lotus" can be seen metaphorically opening in the jeweled uppermost section of the staff.

What does this seemingly ubiquitous symbol actually depict? Two plumes of energy curled in a lovers' embrace? Most certainly, and yet more. Nearly everyone remembers the standing wave of physics from their high school classes; the particles that make up the waveform follow the same path again and again, so that the wave seems to stand still, a static shape composed of moving particles (figure 11d). It is important that we keep this concept of the standing wave in mind because in the next section we take this idea from the two dimensional to the three dimensional.

A common mistake, when looking at drawings of the chakras of Eastern mysticism and their corresponding nadi, or "channels," (figure 13) is to think of them as being two dimensional; such is

---

4. Most likely through the Neoplatonic school of philosophy.

Fig. 12. The staff of the patriarch in the Eastern Orthodox Church bears the images of the coiled serpent and the "thousand petalled lotus." Paintings of patriarchs, like these, are common in Eastern Orthodox churches.

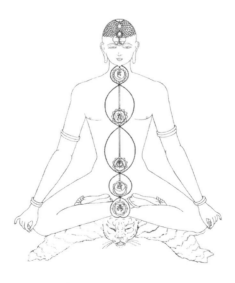

Fig. 13. A two-dimensional representation of the chakras and nadi

not the case. Like the caduceus, these representations in fact depict the two energies entwined around each other in a three-dimensional helicoid. When drawing the nadi and chakras on wall paintings in simplified form, however, the artists of India and Tibet opted for a two-dimensional view as easier to draw and comprehend.

In fact, the DNA strand itself has this very shape, a doubly entwined helicoid around a central axis:

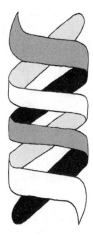

Fig. 14. The strands of DNA

What does all this mean? Is it mere coincidence? We have discussed the fractal Universe and stated that what occurs macrocosmically must occur microcosmically. I am convinced that what establishes our being (our personality, our physical capabilities, our very soul if you will) is nothing more or less than a standing wave in the yin field. This wave replicates itself fractally, initially taking shape in the yang field of space-time within the DNA of the embryo that is to become our body. As we grow older, this wave is still with us, and makes up a network of peaks and nodes that are the nadi and chakras of our yin substance.

For a moment, let me mire in the bog of perplexity those skeptics who read these words with derision. I doubt that anyone in their right mind would question the high technical standards of the ancient Greeks—their mathematics, architecture, arts, and writings are still the foundation on which Western culture resides. The Parthenon is still *de rigueur* for anyone studying architecture; it was built close to 2,500 years ago, but even in its ruinous state today, it takes your breath away. The Greek language is in itself equally mathematical and extremely descriptive. For example, the Greek word for truth is *alithia*; the prefix *a-* is a negative, meaning "not," and the word *lithi* means to "forget," so *alithia* means "that which is not forgotten." The reasoning behind this is simple: It is an inherent human trait to forget a falsehood (because it is not real), and to clearly remember something that has actually transpired.[5] How many of us have been caught telling lies by forgetting the fabrications we have created? I for one am guilty as charged.

Appropriately, the Greek word for evolution (or development) is *exelixis*. The word means, quite simply and unquestionably, "from the helix."

How did they know about the helical strands of DNA, lacking our modern technology? That they were aware of them seems clear. Both the word *exelixis* itself and the fact that the staff of Asclepius, god of medicine, depicts a helix entwined around a central axis (the snake is representative of a standing wave), corroborate this thesis. I believe that the ancient Greeks discovered the helix within themselves through meditation, first contemplating the matrix of larger standing waves that comprise our seven main chakras and then focusing awareness to smaller and smaller levels *ad infinitum*, in this way revealing the fractal microcosm within our being.[6]

Now I will gleefully make things worse and trouble the reader

---

5. While it is well known that people conveniently shield themselves from the truth by forgetting it, this is unconscious denial rather than the normal state of affairs.

6. Perhaps the opposite holds true as well and the universe follows helical evolution macrocosmically.

further by posing the following question: How is it that we as individuals physically exist? Contrary to the expectations of Descartes, the body's cell structure is not a constant and mechanistic thing; rather, cellular biology is somewhat like quantum theory. Our bodies are in a uniform state of flux, cells dying out and being replaced every second. The pancreas, for example, replaces all its cells every twenty-four hours, while the stomach replenishes its cells every three days. The body's white blood cells are renewed every ten days, while 98 percent of the protein-based tissue in the brain, that most complicated and wonderful of organs, is replaced once a month. What is it that keeps us in one piece? Perhaps the only thing that defines our being is something like a computer program in our autonomous nervous system, telling our bodies to replace a given cell at a given moment in time so that form and function may be maintained.

And there is more to be discovered here. I have a bone spur in my elbow—it is inefficient, painful, and hinders function. Yet I have had it for more than twenty years. It is not the result of normal aging, but rather was caused by an injury I received as a young man. My body replaces cells and makes use of minerals by the second, as we have seen, so why does it maintain this bone spur? What is it that keeps it there? Theoretically, it could have been dissolved long ago. If my body's sole function were my efficient survival, it should have done away with the injury, instructing other cells to remove it. Yet it has not. For some reason this injury has been programmed into my matrix and has become an irremovable part of myself.

I believe that the so-called computer program maintaining our existence is a standing wave in the yin field, a standing wave that mirrors itself both in our DNA and in our autonomic nervous system, reaching into every cell in our body.[7] This wave is a reflection of our *karma*.

---

7. I have often wondered why medical associations spend millions trying to figure out how acupuncture works when the answer is obvious: Assuming that our bodies are nothing more than a program established in our autonomic nervous system, then acupuncture interfaces with that program, writing a subroutine to address key commands. There is nothing mysterious about this—Chinese medicine is based on the process of continual change, not the details of primary anatomy, as is our Cartesian-based Western medical system.

The macrocosm reflects itself in our nervous system on many levels. Yin and yang interact continuously in that magnificent central computer, our human brain. In fact, understanding this process offers the key to many special functions of our nervous system, including the cornerstone of the practice of nei kung: meditation.

FINITE AND INFINITE

Before we get into anatomy, however, let me reiterate a concept I have presented repeatedly: *The yin energy is beyond space and time, and yet it is continuously a part of our being* (figure 15). In short, each of us is a living, breathing wormhole in the fabric of space-time.

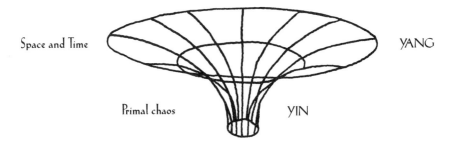

Space and Time　　　　　　　　　　　　　　　　　　　　　　YANG

Primal chaos　　　　　　　YIN

Fig. 15. Yang and yin energies in our bodies

The philosopher Plato himself wrote that "the finite and infinite are inherent in man."[8] To fully understand the implications of this statement we are going to have to touch upon the workings of the central nervous system. Much research has been done in the past fifty years on the physiology of the human brain; we are now in a position to identify the location of specific functions and to operate on the organ as necessary. We know, for example, that the frontal

---

8. Plato, my translation. The idea of an infinite and formless chaos (χάος, "that which gapes open"), coexisting with the finite (πέρας) was a central part of ancient Greek cosmology.

lobes govern most analytical decision making, while the cerebral hemispheres in general handle sense and movement. We know that the brain stem controls heartbeat and breathing, while the cerebellum directs balance and muscle coordination. Finally, the hypothalamus regulates body temperature and the release of hormones.

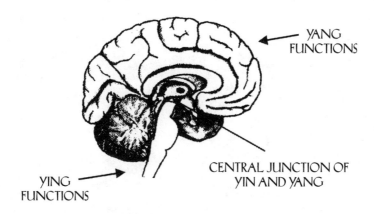

Fig. 16. Yin and Yang in the human brain

This is not an anatomy book, and I am not a neurosurgeon, so there is no point in delving deeper here. What matters is that the central nervous system governs both conscious and unconscious action, or, in other words, both yang and yin. Phrasing it differently still, we could say that the central nervous system supervises things both physical and metaphysical; it is the understanding of yin and yang that allows us to glimpse this (figure 16).

Much has been written lately about it being possible to sense a spirit's presence by feeling a cold shiver on the back of your neck, and Hollywood has certainly picked up on this telltale signal as well. I'll admit to having had the same experience myself, so let's say for a second that spirits do exist and that such a reaction is a physiological response to their presence—how can we explain it?

I believe that it can be readily explained if we accept that the lower brain stem and spinal cord are connected to the yin field of existence (and as such can "touch" a yin entity), while the cerebral cortex is yang.

This makes more sense if we accept that our evolution (*exelixis*— "from the helix") has occurred progressively from the yin field to the yang field over the eons. Life began in the oceans (water is a yin element) as single-cell bacteria and progressed onto land. Our brain stem is still a remnant of our time as reptiles, and it is well known that we can witness our evolution in the development of the human embryo.

If I am correct in stating that the lower brain stem and spinal cord are connected to yin energy, that would mean that we are all interconnected by a field of "dark" energy that binds our unconscious minds together. Indeed, I am convinced that Carl Jung was right, and that the human mind is separated into conscious, personal unconscious, and collective unconscious functions.

What does this mean? Until very recently, it was thought that the neurophysiological mechanisms serving personal awareness reside in the cerebral cortex. But now anatomists are under the impression that the cortex serves to integrate sensory input and organize motor patterns, while the consolidating focus of the nervous system itself may be a part of the brain stem called the reticular formation. This conclusion was derived from studies of the electrical activity of the brain recorded with an electroencephalograph.

Therefore, our awareness must be both yang and yin, conscious and unconscious; we are microcosms of the Universe, images of eternity, so this must hold true. The reticular formation is simply one area where yin and yang energies interact. Perhaps, remembering that we create things in our own image, the following metaphorical illustration will help us better understand human consciousness.

The home personal computer is a common instrument that will become more powerful and more prevalent with each passing year. Still, some things will remain consistent. The functioning of a personal computer is based on three basic ingredients: hardware (the circuitry that makes up its body), software (the programming that gives it its capabilities), and some form of power, such as a battery or electricity, to make it all work. These three components are inter-connected, and all serve to drive the computer; it is ridiculous to talk of software without hardware to lend it form or electricity to drive it.

Since we unavoidably create things in our own image, it must be understood that we are like that computer in the end. We, too, have hardware—our bodies. We have software—the "programming" or input that has made up our personalities since birth. And finally we have bioenergy—the "electricity" of life, the as yet unidentified force that fuels our existence and still baffles scientists.

A computer program cannot exist independently of a physical medium; we must use some means of transport (a disk, CD, DVD, and so forth) to carry it around. Can our software (our personalities) exist independently of our hardware (our bodies) and our electricity (ch'i)? I will try to explain how such a thing could occur. But my reasoning will not please everyone – it is more Taoist than Judeo-Christian, I am afraid.

First, we have disproved the Cartesian concept that our person-alities are somehow independent of our bodies; it would be wonder-ful if this were true, but we know now that this is not the case. An injury to the brain will completely change the personality of the individual—this phenomenon has been observed again and again in today's hospitals. And even stranger occurrences have been docu-mented under clinical conditions in recent years. For instance, heart transplant patients receiving a donor heart will often develop the tastes—likes and dislikes—of the late donor. There is no logical rea-son for this under our current biophysical model. And in essence, these unexplainable complications of the transplant process confirm an axiom postulated by the sages of the Orient for millennia: *We think with our bodies*. Every cell in our body plays its role in formulating our personality; our mind is not limited to or confined by our brain.

Perhaps we should look at things from a more Eastern perspec-tive to understand this; in this instance I am referring to early Christianity (which we have conveniently forgotten is an Eastern religion). Following the initial spread of Christianity, the literally hundreds of interpretations of the teachings of Christ, as we have seen, led to the institution of the Ecumenical Councils, which defined dogma acceptable to the reigning religious and secular authority of the time. When the subject of One God as Trinity came to be debated, a particularly astute individual, the bishop Spyridon (later canonized as a saint—and this one really was!), came up with the metaphor of a brick to explain how one thing could be composed of three essences. A brick, he said, is composed of earth and water and fire (it is baked in an oven), and yet is one thing. With this metaphor he portrayed the Trinity in a concrete, rational manner that others could comprehend.[9] Perhaps we should consider ourselves as that brick. We, too, have a physical form (the earth in the brick); we contain water (the standing wave in the yin field that defines our essence); and we are driven by fire (bioenergy, ch'i, the breath of the cosmos). All three are interrelated—each one connects with and influences the others in order to create the brick. Add too little earth, and the brick will not be sturdy. Add too little water, and it will be brittle. Finally, be remiss in baking it, and it will turn to crumbly mud. All three components are necessary to create the brick. Similarly, affect our body, and you affect our soul. Modify the amount of energy that the body and soul receive, and you transform both as well. Finally, transmute the standing wave that defines our awareness and you affect both the physical body and the energy it can contain. (This is what my own master has achieved). All three elements of our being are necessarily interdependent.

So what do I mean when I say that our souls live on after death? To continue with our earlier computer metaphor, we are born with an initial program; whatever has caused us to be born as we are gives us something to start out with—tendencies, inclinations, and talents. From that point on, we are like blank disks greedily storing input and data with each passing day. In time, our major operating system is established. And then what? When the time comes for us

---

9. Of course, the Party Line is that when he spoke that metaphor, the brick miraculously, through the grace of God, separated into its components and then reformed itself for all to see.

to pass on, is that program—all that we have hoped for, loved and hated—gone?

Of course it isn't. But neither is that program entirely functional. It is like a recording on a CD-ROM; while it does exist, it can do nothing by itself, lacking a means to operate.

In order to explain this concept, we must return to our anatomy. I suggested earlier that both the yin and yang energies express themselves in our nervous system, and that this means that we are continually in contact with the primal chaos that existed before space-time. Let's say that our cerebral cortex and other parts of the cerebral hemispheres are yang, and that the brain stem and spinal cord are yin. The standing wave, the fractal computer program that defines us, permeates our entire body, and this is something we will see to be crucially important further on. For now, let's concentrate on the yin field. We have said that space and time do not exist in that primal chaos. What that means is that *in that place the awareness of each of us is interconnected with the awareness of all others*—we are, in fact, part of one mass consciousness, as Jung predicted.[10] To get back to the example of the personal computer, we could say that we are all coupled by modem to a gigantic Internet recording every action we have taken and every thought and emotion that has become a part of our personal unconscious. (I personally believe that our brain "uploads" files into the mass unconscious during R.E.M. sleep.) In space and time, while we are alive, we have the ability to create, to think analytically, to dream, to lie and fabricate. This is because we possess both the yin and yang energies, both conscious and unconscious capability, while living. However, we do not retain this ability to create and analyze when we pass on; indeed, at the most basic level we are little more than a recording of what has transpired, possessing fundamental instincts and desires but not much more. Spirits are

---

10. The *collective unconscious* was a term introduced by the psychiatrist Carl Jung to represent a form of the unconscious mind common to humanity as a whole and originating in the innate structure of the brain. Like many great men, Jung was ahead of his time; had he lived in our day and age, with the prevalence of personal computers and Internet access, he likely would have proved his theories without difficulty.

yin; they lack the ability to "feel" the softer emotions, which is a yang trait. But they do remember. And they can still watch, observe, and record.

I do not pretend to know what happens to us when we die. Whether we live one life or reincarnate is not for me to say. But I do know that we continue on, and I do know that, for a length of time commanded by whatever forces in the Universe govern such things, each of us will exist as the simple spirit described above.[11] Like a CD or a videotape, every part of us is there, waiting.

There are exceptions, though, to this rule: If the spirit has brought yang energy with it in its passing, it can affect the physical world and retain conscious thought to a great degree. The decision to bring yin and yang together in the spirit through a process of meditation undertaken exclusively while the individual is alive changes things considerably. In essence, this practice is nei kung, the development of inner power.

Devotees of Eastern thought will use this model to justify and promote the concept of karma, stating that the recorded "vibration" (standing wave in the yin field) described leads to subsequent reincarnation. Perhaps, but this model can be used to justify the Christian or Muslim philosophy as well. For example, one could say that should an incarnate deity choose to make a second coming and resurrect those departed souls he judges worthy, all he would have to do is restore yang energy to each specific vibration. After self-replicating fractally, these oscillations could restore the human beings in question. Who knows? I personally would not dare to judge any belief system; I believe we are too finite to judge the actions and intentions of the Infinite.

But let us move away from the afterlife for a time and return to this one. Accepting that our nervous system processes the yin energy and accepting that this yin energy is the primal chaos beyond space and time explains such phenomena as telepathy, synchronicity, and remote viewing. If we possess the innate capability to go "online,"

---

11. In *The Magus of Java* I described several encounters with human spirits.

then all we have to do to "communicate" is to do so consciously. Unfortunately, this is not as easy as it sounds—imagine, for a moment, all humanity as the fingers of a single hand, with each finger being attached to the palm but for some reason unaware that this is the case. But as we develop our meditational perception to greater levels, we can descend deeper into the mass unconscious, and develop our awareness of *hyperconsciousness*.[12]

I will close this chapter by returning to the objections lodged by that dear lady whose acquaintance I made through my friend Spiro. The purpose behind the anatomy lesson outlined here is to give you an idea of the physics of spirituality. While I do believe that it is possible to pass on capabilities from master to student with a simple touch, one must be careful to distinguish power from compassion and, further, from enlightenment. It would be wonderful if all individuals with power had good intentions and had achieved enlightenment as well, but this is often not the case. Frequently, power serves little more purpose than to enlarge the failings of the teacher. I have met individuals with extraordinary telepathic abilities posing as divinely inspired teachers, when they in fact had the emotional and mental foundations of the average teenage adolescent. This chapter should help you see how such a thing is possible. Pyrotechnics aside, many masters may not be at all capable of directing their students on a path of true enlightenment. Be wary therefore when you shop; the packaging does not always define the product.

---

12. *Hyperconsciousness* is as good a word as any. When individuals reach this state they are aware of everything around them and yet still very aware of themselves.

Chapter 4
SPHERES

While living as a hermit in the mountains, you cannot get good coffee.

Kosta's Rules of Mastery, number seventeen

It was a cold afternoon, and I walked briskly through the misty streets of Athens, a tall man clad in gray. I choose to be unobtrusive whenever I can, in imitation of my master, and so typically wear gray clothes (to my chagrin they were in fashion that winter). It always astounds me that no one looks twice at John as he passes. People do not suspect that a man with the power of a god is walking by—John is that unassuming.

I, simple mortal man that I am, rank beginner despite my age and experience, have managed at least in my time with this immortal to learn the virtue of humility. Life's little lessons, a reflection of my master's teachings, have managed to beat the arrogance out of me. And so I seed to remain inconspicuous wherever I go. It is a practice that has served me in good stead.

On that particular day I was on my way to a meeting with a good friend, Karolos, a t'ai chi chuan instructor and corporate CEO with whom I shared a common interest in kung fu.[1] Karolos is a student of the headmasters of both the Chen and Wu styles[2] of t'ai chi chuan and

---

1. John Chang's genealogy is called Pa L'ei Chuan (Eight Ways Thunder Boxing) and, as a kung fu discipline, combines both Taoist and Shaolin Buddhist teachings.
2. He is a student of the masters Chen Xiaowang and Wang Peisheng respectively.

has a degree in physics along with a wildly successful corporate ca-
reer. Like myself, he is a product of our century, a child of a cultural
convergence that had matured with the millennium. People like us are
neither East nor West, but both—children of the world.

More important for me at the moment, he had also learned
through various trials and tribulations in life to value a good cup of
coffee, and savored exercising his gray matter while consuming it.
For the record, neither of us really smoked—but I had learned, in
my brief time in the mountains, to appreciate the little comforts that
civilization provided us. They are indeed the most significant.

I entered the sidewalk café where we had planned to meet and
shook the drizzle from my arms. The waitress sized me up; the scales
dipped in my favor (my clothes were plain but neither shabby nor
unkempt) and she seated me with a smile. I studied the people around
me: businessmen battling their peers for a daily wage, stockbrokers
trying to keep up with the horse race, young girls whispering to their
lovers on their cellular phones. I was out of place in this society, a
throwback to another time, a former engineering manager whose life
and outlook had forever been altered by contact with a separate reality. Still, I love the hustle and bustle of the city, the dance of people's
passions and fears, the interplay of desire and magnanimity. Civilization is wonderful and I could not readily give it up.

Shaman, the King of the Mountain had called me, asking for help
in my surreal dream. I had tried to aid him, though the mining cor-
poration that assailed his kind had resources beyond my wildest
dreams. Still, I could not be completely honest with the ecological
groups I contacted in my attempts to assist—if I told them that earth
spirits required their help; they would have laughed their socks off.

Shaman. I was *not*. I did not have the gift. Whatever skills I had were
the result of perseverance and discipline. Neither was the way of spirits
my chosen path. I was something else, a scholar with an open mind and
the burning desire to glimpse reality. Beyond that, I was nothing, a babe
lost in the wilderness, struggling to make his own way.

Karolos walked in, speaking on his cell phone. As a corporate
CEO, he was continuously pressed for time, but he still managed

somehow to cope with the workload and continue his training in t'ai chi chuan. Elegantly dressed and charming, he won an immediate smile from the waitress, who escorted him to my table; she was expecting a good tip, I gathered.

I had first met Karolos under the simplest of circumstances. After reading an article of his on t'ai chi in a local magazine, I decided that the man knew what he was talking about and simply called him up. We had become friends very quickly, sharing the same overall restlessness and an enthusiasm for esoteric martial arts.

I found as well that he shared a willingness to trust his own eyes and ears and not shy away from the improbable. This faith of his probably saved his youngest son's life. I had known Karolos and his wife, Irene, for a few months when their youngest, David, was born; the child was sickly from birth, and spent the subsequent year in and out of the intensive care ward. It was on a visit to their home with Doris, in an attempt to console them, that I first felt the prickling of something hostile afoot.

"Irene," I asked, "before David was born, did anything strange happen around the house?"

"It's interesting that you should mention it," she said. "Yes, there was an unusual incident. We had a table with a marble top . . . and inexplicably, in the middle of the summer, the tabletop suddenly cracked in half and fell to pieces."

"Are you sure the other kids hadn't been monkeying with it?" I asked. They had two other boys.

"Yes. We were all sitting in the living room when it happened. It was so loud that it scared us, almost as if the tabletop had exploded."

"What do you suspect?" Karolos asked me.

"Yin power," I said. "There is yin energy pouring through this house. From what, I cannot say."

"You think it's a spirit?"

"Could be. If it is, it's a bad one."

Karolos did not hesitate, scoff, or ignore the warning. The next morning he called friends in China who in turn loaded a crate with talismans from the White Cloud Monastery in Beijing. Within two weeks the charms arrived in Greece and Karolos immediately installed them in a perimeter around his home. Almost at once, David was out of the hospital for good, and grew to be an amazingly frisky and powerful little boy. He is still my favorite of Karolos's brood.

My friend sat down at our table, relaxing into the chair. We ordered two obligatory cappuccinos.

The initial topic of discussion was a nonprofit organization we had just formed and named The Wenwukuan. *Wen* is Chinese for "culture" or "learning," *wu* are the martial arts, and *kuan* means "society" or "house." Thus *wenwukuan* means "society combining culture with the martial arts." But the implications of the name we chose reach far beyond a simple translation of its root words. *Wen* (culture) in our organization's name also includes science, in this case Western science; *wu* includes esoteric martial arts, hence Eastern mysticism. The Wenwukuan is not just a joining of East and West, but is focused on the research of every attempt man has made, throughout history and throughout the world, to link technical knowledge with yogic discipline. The reader should not, however, deem that there is anything tremendously original in the effort. We are Greeks and such undertakings are as old as Apollonius of Tyana.[3] (See appendix 1, note 1.)

We are very lucky to be living in this day and age, though—in millennia past, such research as ours had demanded the armed progression of one of the greatest conquerors of all time, Alexander of Macedon. King Alexander had thrown open the doors between East and West, using brute force—and, though perhaps all he was interested in was a good fight, he had more than served the world in his pursuit of glory. As I sipped my cappuccino I said as much to Karolos, comparing the Hellenistic Age to our global one.

---

3. A Pythagorean yogi who lived in the first century C.E. and whose story has been suppressed because it portrays a figure much like Christ in temperament and power. Please refer to appendix 1 for further details.

"This is our second chance," I said. "Another great opportunity."

"You're dreaming," he said. "Globalization in our day and age is a product of financial manipulation, nothing more."

"That's always been the case," I replied. "The Silk Road was instituted by merchants, but that didn't prevent ideas from being transferred from China to England and vice versa.[4]

"True. And the amazing thing is that just as information is provided by the Internet today, the dissemination of knowledge then was felt on all fronts almost immediately. Especially in philosophy and religion."

"For instance?"

"Well, the Stoics, for example. Did you know that they believed in bioenergy, just like the Chinese and Hindus?"

The Stoics made up a school of philosophy that flourished in late Greek (Hellenistic) and Roman antiquity. It has been defined as "one of the loftiest and most sublime philosophies in the record of Western civilization."[5] An interesting point with regard to the Stoics is that among them were both a former slave (Epictetus) and a Roman emperor (Marcus Aurelius).

"It doesn't surprise me," I replied. I had studied their moral teachings but not their cosmology. Anyway, we know that Greek philosophers went to India to study there right after Alexander's conquests.[6]

"Yes, but it's fascinating that the Stoics believed in ch'i, isn't it?"

The Stoics called ch'i *pneuma* and believed that it governed both body and soul. The word *pneuma* means "wind" or "breath" in Greek, and can be found today in the English word *pneumonia*. The Roman Stoics

---

4. Today people have conveniently forgotten that in the first century B.C.E. goods flowed from as far away as China, India, the steppes of Russia, the fjords of Norway, the jungles of Africa, the Highlands of Scotland, to every city around the Mediterranean. And where trade was instituted, could ideas be far behind?

5. *Encyclopedia Britannica* Online.

6. The philosopher Pyrrhon, who accompanied Alexander, became a student of the Digambara (sky-clad) Jain sect, while Alexander himself was overawed by a guru of the same sect whom the Greeks called *Kalanos*, who followed him back to Persia. (It should be noted that many scholars are now of the opinion that these yogis were not Jains at all, but rather an early form of Hindu Naga, the reason being that they were quite militant.)

called the same force *spiritus*—we preserve this usage in the English word *spirits* for strong alcoholic beverages. It is no coincidence that the words *pneuma* and *spiritus* also mean soul or ghost, or that other cultures have preserved the same usage. In Chinese, the word *ch'i* means "vapor" or "breath" (*ki* in Japanese), while the Tibetan word for life force is *rlung*, which means "wind."

I have studied the *Discourses* of the Stoic philosopher Epictetus primarily because many of his moral teachings are similar to those propagated by Mo Tzu, the founder of the lineage held in this generation by John Chang (see appendix 1, note 2). In fact, the coincidences are in many ways quite startling.

Epictetus (55–135 C.E.) was a slave, and his real name is not known. Indeed, *epiktetos* is a Greek word meaning "he who has been acquired." This unknown heritage provides another uncanny parallel with Mo Tzu, whose name means "Mr. Tattoo"—this Chinese sage was branded a criminal, and his family name has never been established.[7]

But the similarities run deeper. The early Stoic school had come up with the doctrine of *cosmopolitanism*, implying that the whole world (*cosmos*) was their city-state (*polis*). This was a radical departure for the ethnocentric classical Greeks, who believed that anyone not a Greek was a barbarian. Epictetus reminded his students that all men are, by nature, brothers, and that the love and consideration of self that all men instinctively possess (called *oikeiosis*) should be extended in an ever widening circle to family, friends, and ultimately humanity as a whole:

> Do not torment others by imposing on them anything you your-
> self would not wish to suffer. If you would hate to be a slave, make
> sure that no one is your slave . . . for virtue is not compatible with
> hypocrisy.[8]

---

7. Criminals were tattooed in ancient China; Mo Tzu suffered this indignity when he was imprisoned for an unknown crime.

8. Epictetus's words (as recorded by Arrian), my translation. The similarity of his words to Christian doctrine commended Epictetus to early Christian thinkers.

But Mo Tzu, too, preached the doctrine of *universality*, stating simply that we should consider the lives of others as our own:

> If men were to regard the cities of others as they regard their own, then who would raise up his city to attack the city of another? It would be like attacking his own. If men were to regard the families of others as they regard their own, then who would raise up his family to overthrow that of another? It would be like overthrowing his own. . . . Such benefits . . . come from loving others and trying to benefit them.[9]

But there is more. Mo Tzu taught that heaven cared for man and distributed justice in due course, and that citizen and ruler alike should submit to Jodo, the will of heaven. And Epictetus, too, taught that there was a God whose will directs the Universe, and that the sage must align himself with the forces of nature.

It should be stated that these beliefs did not imply fatalism. The Stoic sage was encouraged to participate in the affairs of man, in order to effect change. Indeed, the Stoic as a world citizen had a moral duty to play an active role in society, promoting virtue and right action. Mo Tzu took things a step further; he actually used physical force on several occasions to get the point across. Mo Tzu was no armchair philosopher, but rather a brilliant martial artist and military tactician—a warrior-sage. The Mo-ists, in fact, developed mustard gas to defend the cities of weaker states attacked by larger conquering forces.

The emperor Marcus Aurelius, a Stoic for the most part (but a student of the Pythagorean Apollonius as well), also fought a victorious war, in his instance against barbarian and domestic forces threatening the Roman Empire. Like Mo Tzu, he was no armchair philosopher, but was rather a warrior-sage who *acted* when it was needed.

---

9. Mo Tzu, Hsun Tzu, and Han Fei Tzu, *The Basic Writings of Mo Tzu, HsunTzu, and Han Fei Tzu*, ed. and trans. Burton Watson.

"I was tremendously excited when I read that the Stoics knew of bioenergy," Karolos continued, "but I was disappointed to learn that they considered the seat of the body's energy to be the heart rather than the dantien."[10]

"There isn't really a conflict," I said slowly. "My master also considers the heart to be a center of the body's bioenergy. The dantien is simply a warehouse where energy is stored."

Karolos was excited. "He's said that to you?"

"Yes, but it's actually a common concept in the East. John has stated that the heart is important in circulating ch'i throughout the body, the same as it circulates blood. He also mentioned that during a contest between two martial masters, the ch'i of the stronger will attack the weaker person's heart, no matter where that person is struck. If he is hit on the arm or the leg, say, the energy will still run up to the heart and attack that organ. The heart is a major center for ch'i circulation—at least for nei kung as opposed to ch'i kung—though I'm not exactly sure of the details myself."

There are two different types of ch'i circulation within the body. The first relates to the points and meridians made famous by acupuncture—this is the exterior circulation of energy described by the word *ch'i kung*. But there is an interior circulation as well that connects to the dantien, the bone marrow, and the reproductive system. It is this interior circulation that is nei kung, the development of internal power. Somehow the heart plays a crucial role in nei kung. I have described how I inadvertently caused one of my students to suffer a mild heart attack by striking him on the lower right ribs during sparring.[11]

---

10. Karolos's research centered on Epictitus's *Discourses* and the writings of Marcus Aurelius; however, the following book inspired his investigation and provides an excellent summary of Stoic metaphysics: Jean-Baptiste Gourinat, *Les Stoiciens et L'Âme* (The Stoics and the Soul) (Paris: P.U.F., 1996).

11. See *The Magus of Java*.

"You know," I continued, "Tibetan Buddhists consider the heart to be the seat of the soul as well. They say that the 'indestructible drop' rests in the heart channel wheel or chakra."[12]

"Do you think," Karolos asked, "that Stoic and Mo-ist philosophies could have a common source somewhere?"

"I don't know. But it is interesting that the Stoics developed right after Alexander opened the doors between East and West. And it is fascinating to consider how two ancient philosophies, one Greek and one Chinese, could have come up with the same concepts."

"Truth is universal," he said, and smiled.

There was a moment of silence as we both sipped and let out eyes wander around the room. *People always needed silk back then*, I thought. *Silk that came exclusively from China. Hmmm. I wonder . . .*

Karolos continued then by describing the theory behind Stoic energetics and metaphysics in detail. In this area there turned out to be considerable differences between their viewpoint and that of the Mo-Pai.[13]

But then Karolos dropped a bomb.

"You know," he said, "the Stoics considered the soul to be spherical in nature."

I was silent, waiting for him to continue.

"They thought that lesser souls died immediately upon the death of the body," he continued, "but that souls with reason lasted for an indefinite period afterward, floating around the Universe as sentient spheres of energy. These souls endured for as long as space and time itself."[14]

"One of the first things that John Chang taught me," I said, "was that it was important to put yang energy into the dantien, so that we could take it with us when we died. That way, we retained our conscious mind so that we could return to the earth at will, and kept our humanity, as it were."

---

12. Geshe Kelsang Gyatso, *Clear Light of Bliss* (London: Tharpa Publications,1992).

13. Actually, if it hasn't been done, a detailed comparison between the school of Mo Tzu and the Stoics would make an interesting doctoral thesis. Somebody send me a copy!

14. Per Chrysippus's writings. He was headmaster of the Stoic school from 232–204 B.C.E.

Later, I found a passage in the *Tao Te Ching* that articulates the same concept:

> Those who retain their center, endure.
> Those who die but continue to exist are immortal.[15]

"Immortals are people at Level Four and above," I explained, "who have managed to combine yin and yang within their being. Like my master. As for the rest of us, the most we can hope for is Level Three."

"You think that the Stoics had stumbled onto the same process?" Karolos asked.

"My Master once described a soul with yang as a bubble rising through the water, a sphere of yang in the continuum of yin. . . . What do you think?"

"This is bizarre! But from the standpoint of physics, a sphere would be the form that one substance would take when added to another in a nonhomogeneous solution."

"Yes, " I paused. "And there's more."

I had a friend who had made an extensive study of ancient Greek philosophy and how it tied in to the early Christian church. He had found many references to the spherical nature of spiritual beings. In Rhodes, that famous island, there is an ancient altar with a sphere sitting proudly on top (for all to see and few to understand). In addition, nearby churches were decorated with blue spheres— with a cross added above to Christianize the symbol (figure 17). With these examples I began to believe that it was no coincidence that in the Greek Orthodox Church archangels are usually depicted holding spheres.

Perhaps even more shocking is the fact that the icon of the Trinity itself in the Greek Orthodox church showed God the Father holding two artifacts: one, a blue sphere with the complementary cross on top, and the second a staff, which I was beginning to

---

15. *Tao Te Ching*, passage 33.48.

Fig. 17. The sphere had a presence in early Christian symbolism, hearkening to a belief in the spherical nature of spiritual beings. At top and left are examples from churches; at right, a sphere from a pagan altar.[16]

suspect was a simplified version of the caduceus (figure 18).[17] Conceivably, precepts of this sort were introduced into Orthodox Christianity by assimilation from Greek philosophical schools—Plato

16. Photos in figure 17 are courtesy of Mr. Lefteris Saragas and have been published in *Atrapos* no.7, February 1999, Aldebaran Publishers, Athens, Greece.

17. For some reason, the yang ch'i exhibits a blue coloring in higher concentrations. I do not know why.

Fig. 18. God with sphere and staff

himself once made a reference to the gods "being composed of fire, and spherical in shape."[18]

In Tibetan Buddhism, there is a yogic ritual called the *phowa*, the transference of the mind. It is one of the Six Yogas of Naropa. The adept sends his awareness out through the crown chakra at the very top of the head, from where it can be transferred to another form or to another body. Today this yoga is usually taught as a translocation of the soul to the Heavenly Realm of Amitabha, the Dhyani Buddha of Limitless Light, called in Tibetan Oe-pa-me. Amitabha is thought to be a gigantic ball of light more brilliant than the sun, and all those who attain his Paradise are thought

18. Plato makes this statement in *Timaeus*. Most people interpret this section as referring to the stars in the sky, but I am no longer so sure.

to become spheres of light themselves, leaving their karma as human beings behind them.

I discussed all of these associations with Karolos.

"Well," he said, "there does seem to be a common thread through all of this. I suppose we'll leave it to the academics to sort out."

"It has to do with karma," I said. "All of it has to do with using the solar yang ch'i to cut the standing wave in the yin continuum. Such knowledge was once universal."

"Maybe." Karolos smiled. "Just make sure you don't get excommunicated—or worse, shot. These are the Balkans, remember?"

It was hard to forget.

"I believe that all our great advances are due to cultural interaction. I believe that such is the will of heaven," I said.

"Let's hear it."

"One of the principle rules of evolution is this: *The rate of increase in fitness of any organism at any time is equal to its genetic variance in fitness at that time.*[19] In short, the more genetic variation exists in a population, the faster the rate of evolution in that group, and the greater the degree of fitness in the end. This theorem is fundamental, if you believe in natural selection."

"OK, survival of the fittest. We all understand that."

I smiled. "If I ever get shot, it will be because of the idea I just voiced," I said.

Karolos looked puzzled for a moment, and I went on: "You've heard me say repeatedly that I believe evolution is directed, that there is an intent behind the development of the human race. As if a Higher Sentience really wanted humans to evolve on this planet."

"I've heard you use that idea to justify both the speed and the organized manner in which life on earth and our own species appeared and developed."

"Yes, and it's the basic reason why I tend to favor the multiregional model of human evolution more than the out-of-Africa model.

"What do you mean?"

---

19. First expounded by the geneticist R. E. Fisher in 1930, this law has never been refuted. Indeed, it has been experimentally verified repeatedly.

"There are two supposedly contradictory theories as to how human beings came to spread all over the globe. The first says that our species was born out of geographically separate but analogous events that slowly overlapped each other; this is called the multiregional model of human evolution. Basically it comes down to a parent species—let's call him an archaic *homo erectus*, or maybe *homo ergaster*—leaving Africa about two million years ago and spreading throughout the world. It evolved regionally, but each regional expression did not evolve independently—there was plenty of gene flow in between. Globally this species turned into *homo sapiens sapiens*."

"What's the second model?"

"The out-of-Africa theory, which proposes that man evolved into *homo sapiens* exclusively in Africa and then spread all over the globe like a tidal wave beginning about 100,000 years ago. In this model, neither *homo erectus* nor the archaic *homo sapiens* outside of Africa nor the Neanderthals in Europe played a genetic role."

"And you believe in the multiregional model."

"Pretty much. Actually I believe both played a part, because evolution is directed. A while back excavations uncovered a skeleton of a little boy in Portugal with both Neanderthal and *homo sapiens* traits; the multiregionists were cheering loudly for a while with that one. Then mitochondrial DNA analysis seemed to favor the out-of-Africa model again. The jury is still out. Personally, I'm rooting for the multiregional model. Remember, the rate of increase in fitness of any organism at any time is equal to its genetic variance in fitness at that time. So it makes sense to introduce as much genetic dissimilarity into an organism as you can if you want it to thrive."

"You sound like a devout multiregionist to me—why are you saying that both models played a role?"

"Because I believe that roughly 100,000 years ago additional factors were added into the equation to speed things along."

"So what you're saying is that there might have been, for instance, an initial exodus of primordial man out of Africa way back when followed by a more recent tidal wave bearing a specific design criterion—and that African *homo sapiens* mated with all the other evolutionary paragons around, producing modern man."

I grinned. "It's easy to see that you work with engineers on a daily basis! Yes, I think that was the Plan. The intent was to produce as much genetic variance *and* cultural diversity as possible, then bring it all together. The specific design trait we're talking about was introduced to initiate convergence. I happen to believe that this coalescence is still going on, which is why great things happen every time local boundaries fall."

"But if evolution is directed, then there's no reason for the out-of-Africa model to have taken place at all."

I leaned back in my chair for a moment and considered this. "Well, I believe that there *was* a biological initiative to convergence. Everything needs to have a physical fulcrum in the end."

"I think you're just trying to cover your ass . . . but you do have a point."

I reached for my coffee. "It's more than just trying to cover my ass. It's hoping for the best. Because if the out-of-Africa model holds true exclusively, and no other type of humanoid had anything to do with our species, than we are truly a race founded on genocide and extermination."

"What?" Karolos's face communicated that I'd lost him with this thought.

"What do you think happened to the Neanderthals, to *homo erectus*, and to God knows who else if they didn't mate and ultimately merge with *homo sapiens*?"

Karolos fell silent.

"Yes," I said grimly. "That would mean we killed them off or forced them to extinction, much like we are doing with so many other living beings today. And this is why I sincerely hope we are the product of the genetic experiment of a Supreme Being rather than the scions of annihilation. I don't want to think of myself as a virus."

"OK, let's say you're right, and there *is* a Creator God. Why? Why develop us in this fashion?"

"Survival of the fittest. We're so hot to point at natural selection, it makes me wonder why we hesitate to point that finger at ourselves. What makes you think that we're the pinnacle of evolution?"

"I never thought we were."

"Then you're unique—and a realist. Most people think that we're God's gift to the Universe. I don't think that we're anything more than sperm going at a specified task."

He grasped it then and smiled. "You're right, you *are* going to get shot."

"Probably! Most people think that humanity was created to have some kind of dominion over every living thing. Nonsense! There is a stanza in the *Tao Te Ching* that says:

> Heaven and Earth are not humane;
> They regard All Things as straw dogs.
> Hence the Sage is not humane;
> He regards the common people as straw dogs.[20]

"The term *straw dogs* comes from the imitation dogs made from straw that were burned by the Chinese in sacrificial rites. What Lao Tzu is saying is that nature treats all things impartially—survival of the fittest, right? If an antelope is weak, a lion will eat it. And that makes the whole species of antelopes stronger. But we in our arrogance think that this undeniable rule of nature stops with us—we are at the top of the pyramid, we don't have to work for anything. All we have to do is pick the right religion, and we're immortal! How convenient for us."

"So you think that billions of us were born just so that a handful of enlightened souls could evolve?"

"How many sperm do you expend to make a baby? And what the hell is an enlightened soul anyway? . . . But don't you think it's fascinating that Lao Tzu and the Stoics both stumbled onto the same precepts?"

"The spheres! Is it possible that those spheres are enlightened beings?"

"Maybe. Maybe they are. Or maybe they're an intermediate step, souls that are on their way to enlightenment, that have somehow broken free of the chains that bind us. And maybe those who believe

---

20. Lao Tzu, *Tao Te Ching*, stanza 5, my translation.

in reincarnation are right and we have endless opportunities to make it . . . well, for as long as space-time lasts, anyway. It would be horrible if we only had one shot, wouldn't it? But I *do* think that Natural Law applies on all levels—reality is fractal, right?—and that God's plan is to evolve a whole bunch of enlightened souls if He can. I think those spheres symbolize the spirit breaking free from the shackles of death and yet still having power over the physical world. For me, they represent spirits that have carried yang ch'i with them past their mortal end. I believe that the whole hullabaloo—humanity's presence on this planet, our dominance and civilization—is extant so that such enlightened souls can be evolved." I paused. "I would dearly love to be worthy of such a prize," I whispered, "which is why I'm happy to be living in an age of pronounced cultural exchange."

"And what about the love of God for man? Isn't all of this a bit cold?"

"Is it? Look at nature. Are you saying that God loves nature any less than man? There are two forces governing our development. One is Jodo and the second is karma, the consequence of our actions and desires. Karma pretty much comes down to the decisions we all make every day, and it supersedes Jodo because heaven respects our decisions, for better or worse. We're not supposed to become spoiled brats—outside of a few Hollywood films, have you ever heard of an angel coming down from heaven to stop a suicide? We each have responsibility for our own life, perhaps even for past lives, should such a thing as reincarnation be true. But despite all this, my master told me once that there was no love anywhere on this world that could compare with the love of God for man. Only a mother's love for her child comes anywhere close."

"Did Sifu Chang understand this when he came in contact with the Spirit of God?"[21]

"Yes. He used the metaphor of a mother and her child because, as he said, a mother will love and spoil her child even if he murders

---

21. See *The Magus of Java*.

a dozen people a day. She will forgive him anything. This is the love of God for man."

"If he loves us so much, how can he allow the mess we've gotten ourselves into?"

"That's the point—he loves us so much that he will allow us to do whatever we choose, even to walk into annihilation should we so desire. Everything is up to us; we have total freedom to do as we wish, both as individuals and as a species. But we're not completely on our own—we have been granted many gifts to help us along the way."

Karolos leaned away from the table and smiled. "They probably won't shoot you, you know. With ideas like that, they wouldn't want to make a martyr out of you. They'll probably just plant some heroin on you and set you up as a major drug dealer. But I'll visit you in prison."

"Ah! What are friends for?"

Karolos's cell phone rang and he stood to leave. Suddenly, we were back in the hustle and bustle, the stress and grime of the big city. Stepping out of the café, we let the rain fall on our faces for a time, and watched it color the sidewalk as if enough drizzle could wash it away and take us back to simpler days.

Another morning at the Forum had passed.

Chapter 5
THE THUNDERBOLT

It was Sunday, and my mother was trying to get me to go to church.

She was visiting us for a few weeks, and it was incomprehensible to her that a man could spend a month on a mountaintop searching for the divine inside his own being, and yet be disinclined or too lazy to go to church service on Sunday morning. Doris escaped to the backyard on some gardening task or other that was deemed a suitable excuse, and I was forced to endure the full haranguing of my mother's sharp tongue unassisted. I fled to the confines of my own mind, shutting out the sound as much as I could, and tried to focus on the morning paper and the small cup of coffee she presented to me as a sales pitch. Despite whatever powers of concentration I had developed over the years, she was winning; I felt my blood pressure rising. Many well-muscled young men would be wary of so angering me, but mothers are beyond such things and are invincible in combat.

I was saved by the bell, literally. My student Stamatis telephoned, and asked me if I wanted to visit a dead saint.

Immediately I announced to my mother that I would be going to church after all. She stopped, openmouthed, stunned, in mid-verbalization, my counter-attack having taken her unawares and stripped away her defenses entirely. A look of puzzlement passed over her features. Before she could recover, I told her that it would be an evening service at the shrine of Saint Ephraim. She nodded, pleased, and I savored my peace of mind for the rest of the day.

Ephraim was a Greek monk during the years of the Ottoman conquest who had been tortured to death by the Turks. His bones were broken bit by bit, and the death he suffered—drawn out over an entire day—was horrible.

I had been told stories about Ephraim time after time, that he had worked this particular miracle to aid that person's relative and what-not. The monastery housing his relic was not far from the center of Athens, and I always enjoyed being around Stamatis. He and his wife picked me up in the late afternoon and we drove out to the monastery.

On first impression it was not what most of us would expect upon visiting a sacred or religious site. Peddlers and beggars filled the narrow street leading up to the church. Because there were no lavatories present and the church had many visitors, the entire area smelled like a sewer. It was, all in all, very medieval. I was preparing to be disappointed until the moment when, wearing a smile of grim amusement, I entered the church courtyard itself.

The spirit came to me like a battering ram, as they do to many of us who have passed beyond the first level of power. We appear strange to them, you see, with a distinct psychoenergetic makeup, as a man wearing purple polka-dotted clothing and scuba gear and playing the cymbals would appear to you if he walked into your living room.

I felt a strong pressure on my forehead and at the base of my skull and my mind filled with images. The saint was strong— stronger than me! I had to sit down. Stamatis's wife asked me what was wrong, but Stamatis just laughed; he could himself feel the pressure, though to a lesser extent at the time. I introduced myself to the spirit as best I could, explaining who we were and what type of training we did, and was pleased to receive a positive response. I was shown a spot outside the courtyard where my master could summon and speak to the saint—for all to see—when he visited Greece.

Stamatis was happy; he is a devout Eastern Orthodox Christian and is always searching for affirmation of his faith. He has had to go through his own trials and tribulations as my apprentice—in fact, to date, two of my students have resigned from the training, unable to reconcile the strict dogma of their faith with the methods of the Mo-Pai.

Throughout the ages man has always sought union with the Infinite and this quest for the Divine has evolved into many forms and
acquired as many diverse methods. In the process, wars have been
fought, each group of seekers claiming that their chosen method is
the only one for all. Thankfully, the Infinite itself is beyond such
petty bickering. In all major religions an unchanging and limitless
path to the Source has endured, available to each individual blessed
with the faith to uncover it. Perhaps we could say that God is the
same all over the world, but that man, in his wisdom, makes Him in
his own image, depending on the cultural tradition he has grown up
with. But what happens when a person expresses faith in nothing
that he has not experienced for himself?

I myself, product of diverse cultures, have always had difficulty
with the image of God. I've *wanted* to believe in a specific shape and
form of the Absolute so that I could grow closer to it but have found
that I could not bring myself to relinquish my skepticism.[1] When I
was a child, I was enamored of the Greek Orthodox Church and
even became an altar boy. Like Kazantzakis,[2] however, I questioned
dogma as I grew more culturally and socially aware. Not having grown
up entrenched in any one culture and knowing well the history and
failings of every religious authority representing the Divine, I could
not bring myself to believe in the unproven. I suffered as a result.[3]

How could I come to worship the Absolute? I dabbled in all
major religions, but had been discouraged in the endeavor by un-
worthy mentors and the cold, unbiased appraisal of impartiality and
history. Why judge a faith by its exponents, you ask? But how else

---

1. As human beings, in order to grow close to the Absolute, we need to anthropomorphically view It so that Its shape is familiar to us. Rarely can we reach beyond this need.

2. Nikos Kazantzakis, the noted author of *Zorba the Greek* and other masterworks, was excommunicated by the Greek Orthodox Church for daring to portray Christ in literary format.

3. Indeed, this same type of despair has generated a resurgence of paganism both in
Greece and throughout Europe. While attractive, the rituals and disciplines involved in
worshipping the old gods have been lost to time and depredation, and efforts to do so
involve starting from scratch. It is also unfortunate that this worship is sometimes accompanied by a latent nationalism and racism that has no place in our future.

should we judge it? We are human beings; we cannot esteem the Divine except to see how It is reflected in other men. Hence I unquestionably honored all gods for what they were, but did not feel comfortable in claiming an image of the Absolute for my own.

I have told people that I am a Christian in the sense that I believe that personal redemption is feasible for everyone and that universal love makes that salvation possible; a Muslim in the sense that I believe that there is only one God, and that all men are equal under this one deity (a priesthood is unnecessary); a Buddhist in the sense that I believe that the seeds for enlightenment are within us all as an integral component of our DNA, and that we are capable of reaching the Absolute through our own efforts; a Hindu in the sense that I believe that the Divine takes many shapes and forms to reach out to man; a Taoist in the sense that I have borne witness to the incontrovertible reality of both yin and yang energies and the world of spirits.

And I had two traits going in my favor: discipline and compulsion. It was thus that I learned to follow the thunderbolt.

Beyond all dogma, we have seen that the belief in two opposing universal forces is widespread throughout the history and development of our species. It should not come as a surprise then that the method by which these two forces were joined together was also once global in distribution.

My master has taught me that when the two primal forces are squeezed together, a charge of incomprehensible power is generated. This is likened to a thunderbolt falling from heaven. The energy generated at this level is so intense that John Chang himself has fainted twice trying to contain it within his own being. When a yogi reaches this state, he achieves t'ai chi, the supreme configuration that matter can take in our Universe, a form where the infinite (yin) is joined to the finite (yang). As such, one's spirit is immortal, retaining all sentience and emotion even in death. And while alive, the yogi possesses the might of yin and yang combined: the power of the thunderbolt.

It was no coincidence Zeus of the ancient Greeks was the god of thunder as well as supreme lord of the heavens. His full name is

Dias-Zeus. *Dias* (in Greek, ἀίάς) comes from the Greek verb *diaeró*
(διάιρώ), which means "to divide"; *Zeus* (in Greek, Ζεύς) comes from the
Greek verb *zeúgnimi* (ζεύγνύμί), which means "to yoke together." Hence
Zeus is the supreme god who "yokes together those who have been
divided," or to use today's familiar Chinese terminology, the god who
joins yin to yang.[4]

In the *Orphic Hymns* we find this ode to Zeus:

> First conceived was Zeus, and last shall he exist . . .
> From Zeus are all things created.
> Zeus was born male, Zeus is the eternal woman . . .
> Zeus supports both the earth and the star-filled sky . . .
> He is fire and water, matter and ether, night and day.
> All things reside in the body of Zeus.[5]

The student of Taoism will recognize the multiple references to
yin and yang in this stanza, and recognize Zeus as the state of t'ai
chi (commonly translated as "the supreme ultimate").

Many readers may know of Vajrayana Buddhism, and the fact that
the term has been translated into English as "the Diamond Way." The
Tibetan *dorje*—in Sanskrit *vajra*—(figure 19) has become a popular symbol in fashionable circles, with more and more artists and scholars
turning to Buddhism these days. In actuality, however, the Sanskrit
word *vajra* means "thunderbolt," not diamond, and so Vajrayana means
"thunderbolt path." It should be noted that I am not referring to lightning; the thunderbolt itself is not limited to the electrical energy
produced during its generation.[6] The thunderbolt is a unique
phenomenon whose existence has only recently been examined by

---

4. There are those who will argue this point linguistically, saying that the name uses *Zeus*
for nominative and *Dios* for genitive, but that is not the case. *Zeus* has the genitive Ζήνός
in the same form. Besides, that would be like using Kosta for nominative and George for
genitive—it's just not done.

5. Orphic hymn number 6, collected by Proklos and written in his commentary on Plato's
Timaeus. The translation and presentation are my own.

6. It seems that the electrical field is related to the magnetic, which, in turn, is related to
the bioenergetic.

science. Throughout the ages, the vajra became an emblem for self-unification, and symbolized the coming together of many forces, mental and physical, within the human entity.

Fig. 19. The Tibetan *dorje* (*vajra*—"thunderbolt"— in Sanskrit)

If it is not lightning, what then is a thunderbolt? In Greece we have the following legend: Where lightning strikes the ground, a thunderbolt (*keravnovóli*) will rise to the surface within forty days. According to tradition, this is a long, double-pointed stone that resembles the dorje made famous by Tibetan and Mikkyo Buddhism. In truth, however, the thunderbolt, like the vajra, can take several shapes and has a variety of forms. Modern science calls these stones *fulgurites* (from the Latin *fulgur* for lightning)—they are glassy, tubular, silica minerals fused in the heat from a lightning strike. In figure 20a, Zeus, the Lord of the Heavens can be seen holding such a thunderbolt in his hand,[7] while figure 20b shows the thunderbolt on a third-century B.C.E. coin—the similarity to the Tibetan dorje is remarkable, isn't it? Figure 21 shows the real thing, a thunderbolt collected by a shepherd and given to my friend George (the same

---

7. The statue dates to the fifth century B.C.E. and can be seen in the Athens Archaeological Museum.

man who built the cabin in the mountains).[8] A Tibetan lama once told George that, according to their tradition, when such artifacts are found, they are taken from the ground with a specific ritual to ensure benevolent influence.[9] The most powerful stones are shaped like a dorje. The thunderbolt could have been the basis for Thor's hammer in Teutonic mythology as well.[10]

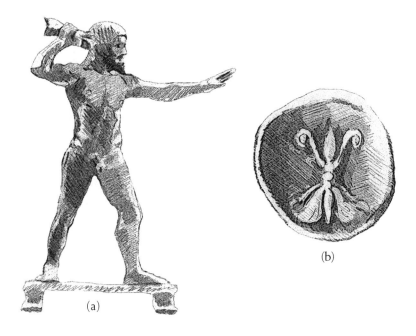

(a)

(b)

Fig. 20. Zeus holding a thunderbolt (a); third-century B.C.E. coin with the image of a thunderbolt (b)

---

8. In Greece there are multiple legends surrounding the thunderbolt *"keravnovóli"*—one should be very careful in handling these objects. Tradition says that they should be placed in the basement inside a sack of grain so that food is never in short supply.

9. That lama would be Kenpo Thupten of the Karma Kargyu Buddhist lineage, who maintains a dharma center in Nice.

10. It is interesting to note that the Hindu god Indra is often called *vajrahasta* (thunder-in-hands). There are indications that the ancient Indians, like the Greeks, the Norse, and the Tibetans, knew of the thunderbolt as a physical object.

Fig. 21. A fulgurite

Fulgurites were symbolic to ancient peoples in that they represented the coming together of universal forces, the sky (yang) meeting
the earth (yin). This process can be duplicated inside our body
through a combination of meditation and breathing exercises; this is
what the seekers who developed the Vajrayana, or "Thunderbolt
Path," stumbled upon. By causing the two opposing universal forces
to meet and coexist, an impermeable "something" not subject to
entropy is generated (hence the use of the term "diamond" for the
vajra). Here, once again, we are applying the principle of *that which
exists macrocosmically exists microcosmically.*

GATEWAYS TO ETERNITY

The supreme Buddha of the Vajrayana lineage is called *Vajradhara*
("thunderbolt and bell"—or, in Tibetan, *Dorje Chang*). He is depicted
with crossed arms, holding a vajra and ritual bell in his hands.
According to Tibetan tradition, the hollow of the bell symbolizes
the wisdom cognizing emptiness; the bell's clapper represents the

sound of emptiness. I believe that the state represented by the Buddha Vajradhara is equivalent to Level Seventy-two of the Mo-Pai training, or the opening of the sahasrara chakra in kundalini yoga, a condition in which emptiness is form and form is emptiness.

In other words, the thunderbolt is achieved first, the union of the infinite with the finite, and ultimately the final chakra at the top of the head, the Thousand-Petalled Lotus, is opened, whereupon the essential nature of the Universe is discovered.

What does it mean to open a chakra? We have talked about the two energies that are the blueprint for our being. To use a metaphor, we can say that every so often these energies tie themselves into a knot.[11] These knots provide a stable base for our energetic makeup, without which the individual would no longer have reason to exist as a human being. There are seventy-two of these knots in our body. The ones along our spine, the main axis of our body, are seven in number and have been made popular by yoga. When a chakra is opened these knots are "cut":

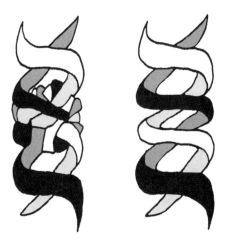

Fig. 22. The "knot" of a chakra before and after opening

11. The actual graphics are quite complex and would require three-dimensional modeling.

More often than not, however, the knot of a chakra is not cut, but rather its void is simply filled, like a cup that is filled with water. (The very center of a chakra is a zero node in a standing wave in the yin field; as such, it can absorb a given amount of yang energy). The cutting of a chakra knot is permanent; once the standing wave is destroyed, it does not reform. The filling of a chakra, conversely, is subject to entropy (see appendix 1, note 3, for details). To better understand what this means, let us use John Chang's method of the Mo-Pai as an example. To do this we must look at the body's main centers as follows:

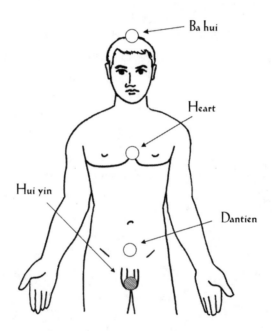

Fig. 23. The main chakra used by the Mo-Pai system

Now, the point at the perineum is called *hui yin*, the "gate of yin" in Chinese. We can take it for granted that the chakra at or near that point (some say at the very tip of the spine) has to do with yin energy—that is to say, it has to do with absorbing the energies of the infinite chaos that existed before our own space-time. Let us say that this spot represents the Infinite. Normal human beings, as yang creatures, cannot tolerate a higher location for this energy center, one that is one step closer to the Infinite; it would drive us insane or kill us.

The first step in filling this chakra is to fill the dantien chakra with yang energy. During training to the end of Level Two, the energetic makeup of the body is enhanced but not altered. I have found what I believe is a classic depiction of this process in my native Greece (an example more than three thousand years old): the statue if the Minoan priestess currently at the Archeological Museum in Herakleion, Crete (figure 24).[12]

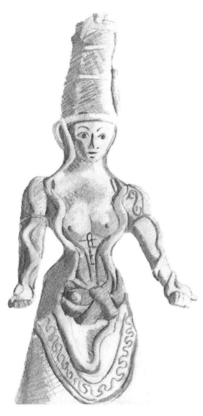

Fig. 24. Statue of a Minoan priestess at the Archeological Museum in Herakleion, Crete

An examination of this statue can be revealing if you know what to look for. Twin snakes can be seen entwined in a knot at her dantien, indicating that she has not severed the cords holding that chakra in place. The evidence suggests that she may well be a practitioner of nei kung—the dantien is the source of her power, which she has managed to raise to the center of her palms. In the Mo-Pai tradition this corresponds to the end of Level Two. At her abdomen can be seen a double helicoid of entwined snakes—though the snakes are quite small—spiraling up to reach between her breasts. This might indicate that the base of her power is still in her lower centers—she has not managed to sever the cords that keep it there. The snake on the top of her hat may signify that the

12. This depiction based on a photo by Leonard von Matt.

energy does reach the *pa hui* point, but that this center is full rather than permanently open. All of these details together suggest that the priestess has finished Level Two but has not progressed beyond this point.

By way of contrast, looking closely at a statue of the sage Bodhidharma in the Victoria and Albert Museum in London we can distinctly see a lotus opening in the area of his dantien, signifying that the chakra has been cut and establishing at once the source of Bodhidharma's great power (figure 25).[13]

We have said that the dantien is the lowest chakra capable of storing yang in the centerline of the human body; the chakra below, the hui yin point, relates strictly to yin energy. When the strands of the dantien are severed, the dantien becomes a mobile ball filled with great amounts of yang ch'i. As we saw in chapter 1, this ball is sent down to the hui yin and essentially modifies the continuum of that point. In the process, the two energies rise together and the state of t'ai chi (the thunderbolt) is established at the former dantien point. In essence, what this means is that eternity itself is one step closer to the individual's personal consciousness.[14]

Fig. 25. Statue of the Bodhidharma in the Victoria and Albert Museum, London

The human being is forever altered at this instant. To use a Jungian phrase, we could say that the mass unconscious and the individual's conscious mind are on an intimate

---

13. The lotus was chosen as the symbol of enlightenment because it is a beautiful flower that rises out of murky waters.

14. If you have noticed a marked similarity to kundalini yoga, you are correct.

basis. He possesses the ability to warp space-time, since that which is beyond space and time is now an intricate part of his being. He possesses superhuman strength and the ability to discharge energy at will. He has become what the Chinese call a hsien, an immortal. He is a child of thunder and wields the power of the thunderbolt.

It is my contention that the process toward this state is as natural as taking a bite into an apple or visiting the lavatory. True, not everyone can become an immortal—but not everyone can run the hundred-meter dash in under ten seconds, either, yet no one seems to doubt that such a thing is possible. Indeed, it is a goal that all sprinters dream of (but few have achieved). To fulfill such an objective, what is required is a combination of discipline and talent—and perhaps the blessings of fate.

Having not found faith in any one religion, then, I made the thunderbolt my path. And I was not alone in the endeavor. As a martial artist, I was happy to discover that the thunderbolt and nei kung itself had been the choice of warriors around the world since the beginning of time.

Chapter 6
THE WARRIOR ELITE

The question of when and where the martial arts began is a subject open to much speculation. In this section, I will elaborate on the origin and evolution of the martial arts based on my own findings and discuss their historic relationship to nei kung. While a mediocre practitioner myself, I have been privileged to train with and win the confidence of some of the greatest living masters in the world, foremost among whom I consider my own teacher. By inclination a scholar and by profession an engineer, I tend to analyze almost everything continuously (a major problem in life, as those similarly afflicted will agree). The martial arts could be no exception. Since meeting John Chang (seven years ago, as of this writing), and having been indoctrinated into nei kung, I could not help but apply what I have learned to researching the history of the martial arts. The conclusions I have come up with may be as seemingly unorthodox as anything else in this book.

Many authors (myself included) have begun similar diatribes with the quotation "The martial arts are as old as man."[1] In fact, they are not. The martial arts are roughly eight thousand years old, and are intimately tied to the evolution of agriculture, property, and the development of edged weapons.

---

1. I really don't know who was the first to use this phrase, but I've managed to trace it back to 1884, when it was employed by Sir Richard Burton in *The Book of the Sword*, in reference to the sword and swordplay. I'm quite sure that brilliant scoundrel swiped it from somewhere else.

In chapter 1, we discussed the comments of Fridtjof Nansen, the Norwegian explorer who, in 1888, was the first modern European to come into contact with the eskimos living on the Greenland icecap. At that time, these people lived much the way their forefathers had, in harmony with nature. Nansen wrote:

> Fighting and brutalities of that sort . . . are unknown among them, and murder is very rare. They hold it atrocious to kill a fellow creature; therefore war in their eyes is incomprehensible and repulsive, a thing for which their language has no word; soldiers and officers, brought up in the trade of killing, they regard as mere butchers.[2]

It seems that nomadic tribesmen around the world, the hunter-gatherers who were our ancestors, lived in a similar fashion, taking from the earth only what they needed. With the establishment of agriculture, we "fell from Paradise," and, to further quote the Bible, "saw that we were naked." Of course, things were not as simple as that; people have been fighting and killing each other for at least forty thousand years, more often than not over food. In fact, many exhumed Stone Age graves have revealed skeletons with flint blades lodged in their ribcages. There are even indications that Neanderthal man was subjected to genocide by his Cro-Magnon brethren. For all that, it is safe to say that war as an institution did not exist before the breakthrough of agriculture, for the simple reason that before we began farming, we really had no concept of property.

For tens of thousands of years men had been hunting with spear and javelin. Prey was struck from a distance—trial and error had shown that it was safer and easier that way. In the initial confrontations between men, the same rule was followed: Get him from far away. But in roughly the tenth millennium B.C.E., two powerful new weapons appeared: the bow and the sling. These new inventions more than doubled the range and impact power of projectile weapons and drastically increased the need for protection. For eight

---

2. *The Enterprise of War* (Amsterdam: Time-Life Books, 1991).

thousand years the bow and sling were the weapons of war. Mobility and cover were as crucial then as they are today. We know that this is so because city walls were one of the first defensive measures devised against invaders; Jericho, for example (built around 8000 B.C.E.), had walls three meters thick and four meters high. The mud-brick houses of Çatal Hüyük in central Anatolia (a middle-Neolithic site) form one continuous wall, and were built without windows or doors (residents entered through a hatch in the roof). Neolithic sites such as these bear testimony to the deadliness of projectile weapons.

It is from the sixth millennium B.C.E. that we have first confirmation of a change in technique, again from the site of Çatal Hüyük. Excavations have brought up a series of daggers made from flint—the blades are broad, pressure-flaked on one side and ground on the other, while the handles are made of bone. One example among them is exquisite, with the handle winding down in the form of a snake (figure 26).[3] This is no butcher's knife, but the ornate and prized possession of a warrior. It was designed for the thrust, and, as such, uniquely fabricated for the personal combat of man against man.

I have my own theory as to how such artifacts came into being. We have discussed the use of projectile weapons. Often wounded enemies were hunted down and executed after a battle, much like archers will track a wounded deer today. No animal dies willingly, and man is no exception; during these assassinations, personal combat was often a necessity.

There were practical considerations to be taken into account: weapons like this dagger were not so easy to manufacture. They require time, effort, and know-how. Knives with wooden or bone handles had been

Fig. 26. The dagger
of Çatal Hüyük

---

3. Michael D. Coe et al. *Swords and Hilt Weapons* (New York: Weidenfeld and Nicolson, 1989).

around for twenty-five thousand years or so, but we have turned up no earlier blades so evidently designed with balance, form, and function clearly in mind. This blade was created by a man who knew how to fight with a knife.

Now, in the early days of organized agriculture, all men were hunters, farmers, and warriors; circumstance and necessity dictated action on an individual basis. But as weapons of destruction became more and more powerful, the need for specialized ability and particular skills developed. Such men as were more inclined and capable to use weapons were the ones for whom they were fabricated. And so the warrior class began to take root, though they would not appear in full bloom until the Bronze Age.

I believe that people back then were less twisted than they are now (civilization has a way of making things both better and worse). The desires and intentions of people, good and bad, were more out in the open. The dagger of Çatal Hüyük cries out its story to me— these warriors, who were not the animals we have come to believe, realized that the bloodshed they were causing was a terrible thing. No doubt their shamans had warned them of the consequences through their spirit mediums. So they tried to keep the fighting among themselves: A warrior fought only a warrior, and they fought by mutual consent. Perhaps there was a large portion of ego involved as well (i.e., "I will fight only those who are worthy"). But that dagger is not a butcher's tool; there are other shapes that lend themselves better to simple execution. A spear, for example, is much safer. Come to think of it, even a stout club is better and less costly to make. The dagger was a warrior's back-up weapon, something that he used in battle up close and personal, a weapon that lent itself for use in a duel between champions.

THE AGE OF BRONZE

We will have to leap forward in time a bit, to the thirteenth century B.C.E., and visit both India and Greece, where the warrior castes held sway in the Bronze Age. It was with the development of bronze that the warrior as an entity really came into being. An alloy of copper and tin, bronze was costly to make, and the raw materials had to be imported from afar. It was rational to distribute such weapons only to those worthy of using them efficiently.

In the *Mahabharata* (traced by oral tradition to 1302 B.C.E.) there are guidelines governing the behavior of a warrior (*ksatriya*) that reflect a code of chivalry reminiscent of the one followed by Arthur and his Knights of the Round Table: Civilians and holy places were not to be attacked during battle, while warriors were encouraged to fight only equals and only for just causes.

The ksatriya nobility practiced a martial art called *vajramukti*, which means "thunderbolt in clasped hands." The word *mukti* essentially means that the fist is shielded and tempered by refinement and culture; it is not indiscriminately applied. In fact, a good way of translating the term would be "the refined fist." (More on that in appendix 1, note 4.)

In the *Iliad*, Hector, first warrior of Troy, belittles Paris Alexandros (who had stolen the beautiful Helen from her husband, Menelaus) and convinces him to duel with Menelaus for Helen's hand. Hector walks boldly up to the armies of skirmishing Greeks and Trojans, shouting to be heard, his spear in a nonaggressive position. He faces thousands of arrows, pellets, and spears at point blank range, but not a shot is fired:

> Hear me, O Trojans and Greeks of the bright greaves, listen to what is offered by Alexandros [Paris], who is the cause of this war. Let the Trojans and Greeks place their weapons on the Earth, which nurtures all things, so that he and the battle-loving Menelaus may duel among themselves for Helen and her riches. He who wins shall claim the woman and her dowry, while all others shall swear friendship and peace among themselves.[4, 5]

---

4. Homer's *Iliad*, rhapsody Γ, my translation from the original; please excuse any errors I may have made.

5. Two points: 1) Note the reference to the Earth "which nurtures all things." Obviously they took ecology a bit more seriously than we do in our day. 2) Yes, they were undoubtedly macho chauvinist pigs, but at least Helen had final ownership of her property. It was inconceivable that her ex-husband could simply seize it, even though she had fled his household and he lived next to her lands.

And Menelaus answers with a roar:

Hear me, for it is I who have suffered the most pain! I think that
now Greeks and Trojans may leave in peace; they have suffered
more than enough because of my grievance with Alexandros, who
began all this. One of us shall meet death, as decided by Fate,
while all of you others shall soon become friends. Bring two sheep
[to sacrifice in oath], a white ram and black ewe for the Sun and
the Earth, and we shall bring a third for Zeus.[6]

We will return to the Bronze Age and the Greeks themselves
shortly, but what is important here is that a code of honor is evident
in the world of the thirteenth century B.C.E., one that ranges from
Greece to India and undoubtedly beyond. These are no bloodthirsty
slayers, indiscriminately slaughtering, but groups of men trying to
live with honor, even fighting among themselves with honor. Such a
code of conduct did not materialize spontaneously—it developed
over centuries. The dagger of Çatal Hüyük suggests that this code
had its roots in the sixth millennium B.C.E. I believe that the amalgamation of warrior and shaman brought it about, and produced the
warrior elite.

I use the term *warrior elite* quite specifically. For example, we know
that writing can be traced back to 3000 B.C.E. in both Mesopotamia
and Egypt, and that it was the creation of the record-keepers of kings.
But accountants cannot hold sway without an army to enforce their
bookmaking, and that means those kings had soldiers aplenty—
soldiers who knew how to fight. And so at this point I must make a
distinction between the soldier, the warrior, and those who made up
the warrior elite.

I should point out that because it contains the root *war*, the word
warrior does not exactly convey the meaning I ascribe to it, but it will
do. I must refer again to the language of the Greeks to present

---

6. What a reference to yang and yin! And it is interesting that a *third* sheep is separately
offered to Zeus, who binds yin and yang together.

concepts clearly; a good example can be found once more in Homer's *Iliad*. The Greek word for war is *polemos* (πόλέμός) which means "to destroy a city."[7] The Greek god of war, Ares, who in turn became the Roman Mars (hence the word *martial*), was not held in high esteem by the Greeks themselves. Indeed, in their culture there was a clear distinction between the *divine warrior* and the *base warrior* who followed Ares and destroyed indiscriminately.

The Greeks had a separate word for "individual combat" as well; Homer uses the word *machi* (μάχή), the meaning of which later came to be broadened to mean "battle" in general terms. It is interesting to note that the word for "knife" is *machaira* (μάχάίρά), which contains the similar root *mach-* (hence the choice of my earlier reference to the dagger of Çatal Hüyük). *Machi* had connotations of honor and fairness that *polemos* did not; the mental image conjured up by the first should be that of two chivalrous knights facing each other in a duel, while that of the latter might be a horde of bandits burning a village and slaughtering the unarmed. Hector uses the word *machi* in his challenge to Menelaus; conversely, he brands Menelaus with the epithet Areifilos, the "friend of Ares";[8] this is a thinly-veiled insult toward one of the men he holds responsible for the onslaught of the war (the second being Paris, whom he also insults, calling him a "pretty-boy capable of nothing but seducing women").

But the ancient Greeks actually had two gods of battle. Along with Ares, whose symbols were the vulture and the rooster, was the virgin goddess Athena, who is of prime importance to our discussion. Athena is the goddess of wisdom and learning as well, and is the patron of scholars and artists. She fights only to defend, and her epithet is Promachos (who fights to protect); her symbols are the olive and the owl. She wears a helmet and armor and bears a shield and spear, but her powers extend beyond space and time, for on her

---

7. From *polis* (πόλίς), "city", and *ollymi* (όλλύμί), "to destroy."
8. I translated Areifilos as "battle-loving" in the earlier section, not having made the explanation above.

shield she carries the image of the head of the Gorgon Medusa, whose visage in life could turn mortals to stone.[9]

Athena represents *alkí* (ἀλκή) the ability to fight not only with bravery but with spiritual power as well. She meets Ares on the battlefield of Troy, and mocks him:

> "Idiot! You still don't comprehend that I am beyond your power, for you dare to face me!" So saying she struck him on the neck and paralyzed his limbs; and Ares falling took up seven acres of land, and his hair filled with dust, and his armor clattered on the earth.[10]

My kind of woman.

Returning to the Bronze Age itself, archaeology has shown us that trade was phenomenally widespread, and that goods traveled from Britain to India (and possibly China) in the fifteenth century B.C.E. or earlier. For example, there are Bronze Age mines for copper malachite ore in France, Britain, Ireland, Spain, Slovakia, Yugoslavia, Austria, and Cyprus. But copper was being used long before the Bronze Age began, so it is to the second main component of bronze—tin—that we must look in order to get an idea of the extent of trade at that time.

Bronze is an alloy of copper, bearing roughly 5 to 10 percent tin. What this means is that bronze-using civilizations must have had access to considerable quantities of tin. But tin does not occur naturally in the Mediterranean, or in Egypt or Mesopotamia. There are some minor deposits in Anatolia, Italy and in Spain—but where did the tin come from that was used in, say, the third millennium bronzes found in the royal graves of Ur and in the city of Susa? We know now that Near-Eastern cities imported tin from the East, most likely from Afghanistan, and trans-European commerce exploited tin

---

9. The Gorgon is symbolic of the powers of the Infinite. Medusa comes from *meta* (beyond) and *ousia* (substance). Hence Medusa translates as "the substance of that beyond."

10. Homer's *Iliad*, rhapsody Γ, verses 405–410.

deposits in Cornwall, England, and southern Brittany in the early second millennium B.C.E. The archaeological record tells us that by the fifteenth century B.C.E., organized, long-distance trading was established throughout the world. This trade linked the far reaches of northern Europe to the southern shores of India, and, I suspect, to places far beyond. We know, for example, that all the amber found in Mycenean and Minoan Greece is of Baltic origin—and we know that ebony and hippopotamus and elephant ivory were moved throughout the world in considerable quantities. And royalty in ancient times often exchanged valuable gifts from far-away locales—hence the presence of Near-Eastern seals and jewelry in Mycenean Greek graves, and vice versa.[11]

Further, trade was democratic, not something reserved just for royalty. As early as the third millennium B.C.E., before the Bronze Age proper, quality stones for use in tools and weapons were traded liberally throughout Europe and the Near East. Obsidian from the Mediterranean, dolerite from Brittany, and flint from England, Germany and Poland flowed around the continent. Pottery was traded from East to West and south to north, and Lebanese wood specifically became known widely as a reliable construction material. Beyond materials, cultural innovations also made their way from place to place: the yoke plow, alcoholic beverages, and the bridle are all prime examples. And one other artifact, something most important to this text, made its way through ancient lands: the sword.

We can trace the existence of the warrior elite through the archaeological record and through myth and oral tradition. The journey of the sword through ancient lands provides strong archaeological evidence.

It seems that beginning with the sixth millennium B.C.E., warriors dueled with spears and shields, and closed with daggers.

---

11. *Gods and Heroes of Bronze Age Europe: The Roots of Odysseus* (Strasbourg: Council of Europe, 2000).

The tomb paintings of Beni-Hasan tell us that wrestling was common in Egypt by 2000 B.C.E.[12] I would guess that this held true throughout the world as far back as the fourth millennium B.C.E. As anyone who has practiced traditional jujutsu knows, wrestling is a component of personal combat with a knife; my guess therefore is that people knew how to use jointlocks, trips, chokes, and throws a good six thousand years in the past (if not earlier). Martial arts employing striking were just as widespread.

Now, copper knives and hatchets had become popular throughout the ancient world beginning in the fifth millennium B.C.E., but to tell the truth, they were more status symbols than they were functionally useful objects; in fact, good quality obsidian weapons and tools were much more effective than copper ones (so was well-napped flint, for that matter).[13] In short, copper weapons, though prestigious and fairly widespread, were not something to get excited about. As copper metallurgy improved, so did copper axes and knives, but it was not until the discovery of bronze that metal weapons suddenly became de riguer.[14]

Bronze weapons were far, far better than their stone counterparts. First to be developed as a weapon of war was the bronze knife, most of which, based on those we have uncovered, were triangular in shape. Bronze was expensive and not available in quantity; its metallurgy was a complex and treasured secret. The second bronze application created by the bladesmiths was a simple extension of the knife: placing a triangular blade at a 90-degree angle to a pole, they thereby

---

12. Michael Poliakoff, *Combat Sports in the Ancient World* (New Haven: Yale University Press, 1987).

13. Copper was useful for ornamentation, as a joining material, and in jewelry in conjunction with gold.

14. Ötzi, the mummified wanderer found high in the Ötzal Alps in 1991 and dated to 3350 B.C.E., carried a copper axe, but one could tell where his real faith lay: He carried a flint knife, a flint drill and scraper, and a bone awl. His main weapon was a 1.8–meter yew bow and fourteen arrows. I think copper axes were much like Rolexes—they're undoubtedly nice, but a Casio G-Shock will take just as much abuse at a fraction of the cost.

created a halberd. Such weapons became popular throughout Europe in the latter part of the third millennium B.C.E. through the middle of the second millennium. A warrior's grave excavated in Poland and dated to 1850 B.C.E. turned up a halberd, a triangular dagger, an axe, and a knot-headed pin and gold spiral, all in good condition (figure 27).

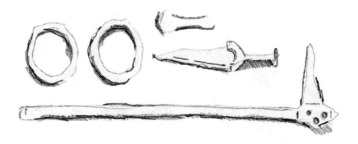

Fig. 27. Artifacts from a warrior's grave in Poland, circa 1850 B.C.E.[15]

Axes became similarly popular, largely because they conserved bronze and were easier to cast. Indeed, for many years they were the weapon of choice, until the arrival of the sword.

It is not from Europe, but from the Near East, that we first find evidence of the sword. Representations of bronze swords with curving blades dating from the third millennium have been found at the early Babylonian dynastic site in Tello. This indicates that Babylonian metallurgists were the first to come up with a technique for casting larger quantities of bronze, and that their bursars were the first to decipher the logistics of moving and refining large quantities of tin.

---

15. These were found in a grave at Leki Male in Koscian, Poland (Únetice culture, circa twentieth to nineteenth century B.C.E.) The artifacts are housed at Museum Archeologiczne, Poznan. The halberd shaft is seventy-two centimeters long, the blade eighteen centimeters long.

In a tomb at Byblos in Lebanon, dating to the early eighteenth century B.C.E.,[16] examples of the real thing have been discovered—swords in good condition (figure 28).

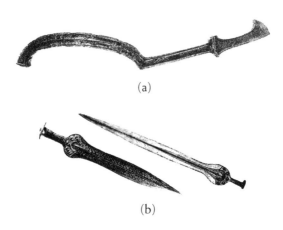

(a)

(b)

Fig. 28. The curved bronze sword of the Near East and western Asia, circa the early second millennium B.C.E. Sketch by Sir Richard Burton (a).[17] The bronze double-edged sword of the West, circa the seventeenth century B.C.E. (b). It is interesting to note Europe's preference for the straight double-edged sword, even in such an early example.

From western Asia the sword quickly made its way into Europe by means of Anatolia, the Aegean, and mainland Greece. By the sixteenth century B.C.E., the bronze double-edged sword, wasp-waisted or rapier-like (figure 28 b), had a similar shape and make throughout all of continental Europe, western Asia, and the Mediterranean basin; it was a treasured artifact whose mythos was to far surpass that of its predecessors, the spear, the bow, and the axe. This relatively rapid dispersion of the bronze sword (a weapon more useful for dueling than for the melee of combat) and the development

16. Coe et al., *Swords and Hilt Weapons.*
17. Sir Richard F. Burton, *The Book of the Sword* (London: Chatto and Windus, 1884).

of a related sword culture can mean only one thing: The warrior elite were already in place, with the highest among them being, unquestionably, masters of nei kung.

CHILDREN OF THE GODS

Beginning with *Gilgamesh*, epic tales of semidivine warriors fighting anything that moved and ridding the land of monsters made their mark in the ancient world, sowing the seeds of the practice that John Chang is even now passing on to me. It's important to note that these are not infallible heroes always on the side of right, but are rather quite human, with great failings and foibles to match their abundant powers. In short, they screw up a lot and have to pay the price. The divine warrior of this ancient time wrestles continuously with his duty to his God, his passion for life, and the lure of base human desire. Hercules, for example, slaughters his own wife and children not once but twice. Samson's story, below, is well known for its lesson on human frailty. The lists are endless; these are indeed humans who are larger than life, but who never stop being human, with all the accompanying failings.

We find the warrior elite firmly entrenched in society by the early Bronze Age; indeed, all warfare at that time was seen as heroic, as shown in the exploits of men retained in epics such as the *Odyssey* or *Gilgamesh*. At times these warriors are more knightly (such as Arjuna in the *Mahabharata* or the warriors who display a kind of chivalry in the *Iliad*), at other times they behave as complete animals (such as Hercules, who cuts off the nose and ears of the herald of Orchomenus).[18]

The Biblical account of Samson[19] is a prime example for those studying the warrior elite and the science of nei kung, providing insight into how these men developed their powers. In Hebrew his name is spelled Shimshon, and means "son of the Sun." Samson was a Nazirite (meaning "he who abstains") and a holy warrior who fought

18. Sorry, folks, but he was far from being the nice guy Kevin Sorbo portrays on the TV series. As a boy, Hercules broke his music teacher's skull with his guitar just because the man dared to criticize his playing!

19. Judges 13–16.

the Philistines during the early tribal period of Israel in Canaan (the twelfth through the tenth centuries B.C.E.).

Everyone is familiar with the tale so there is no need to reiterate it here. The crux, for our purposes, is that Samson possessed extraordinary physical powers, and the moral of his story relates the disastrous loss of his powers after the violation of his Nazirite vows. But how exactly are those vows violated? With his life revolving around his affairs with Philistine women, Samson is depicted in the Book of Judges as being ruled by passion. He is credited with the usual extraordinary feats typical of demigods—slaying a lion with his hands, moving the gates of Gaza, killing a thousand Philistines with the jawbone of a donkey—but he first breaks his religious oaths by "feasting" with a Philistine woman from the neighboring town of Timnah.[20] Samson finally falls victim to his foes through the love of Delilah, a woman of the valley of Sorek, who beguiles him into revealing the secret of his strength. He is captured, blinded, and enslaved by the Philistines, but in the end, through the return of his strength, he avenges himself by demolishing the great Philistine temple at Gaza, destroying, in the process, both his captors and himself.

Now, Delilah (or *Dalila* as is more correct), means "desire" in Hebrew, and with that thought in mind I would like to present a revised interpretation of the Samson epic—one that looks at the story in relation to workings of the power of nei kung.

The "Son of the Sun" is a practitioner of nei kung, for in this story the ancient Hebrews have correctly identified that it is the solar yang ch'i that fuels his great powers. Forgoing wine and uncut hair has little to do with being a Nazirite; these are little more than symbols for what he has really renounced: the pleasures of orgasm and ejaculation. As a practitioner of nei kung, he continuously harnesses his sexuality, bringing that power up and into his dantien center. It is this yang ch'i that gives him his prodigious strength.

Only after hearing from John Chang the stories of past masters of the Mo-Pai, and after practicing nei kung myself, did I under-

---

20. And he is cornered by the thousand Philistines, whom he slayed while in a dalliance with *another* Philistine woman, this one a professional acolyte of men's pleasures!

stand how difficult it is in truth to harness one's sexual powers and live in celibacy. I doubt that there is a practitioner of nei kung or kundalini yoga out there who will not agree with me. As your power increases, so does the strength of your emotion and so do the related passions you might have. Nei kung is an uphill battle.

We all stumble and fall. At my level, I am allowed one ejaculation a month, but I would be lying if I said that I keep to that program rigorously. Sexual desire is a tremendous opponent, in essence the root of life, and living in society makes things that much more difficult. One escape route available is nonorgasmic sex, which loosens the psychological load somewhat. But this approach, too, is quite difficult for both practitioner and partner. Fortunately, the system has a lot of safety measures built into it. For example, during those days that I permit myself one orgasm, I am pretty much at full power by the next morning. Despite this, the regimen says I may not train for three days afterward, and I do not. When I really let myself go, however, and enjoy a night of torrid sex, ejaculating repeatedly, then the gates of the dantien truly slam shut, and whatever benefits I may have garnered from nei kung are lost for a time.

I'm betting this is what happens to Samson. In coupling with Dalila (*desire*), he allows himself to have an orgasm not once but three times, and in doing so, loses all access to his inner power (those Philistine women must have been truly something). He is just like any man when the soldiers seize him and blind him. But his captors do not understand the principles that govern his powers; if they did, they would kill him on the spot. After a time, let's call it a week or so, his power begins to return. Having been blinded and imprisoned, he cannot really train to recover his full strength—indeed, he's likely not able to perform even a simple meditation. As there is not much more he can do to fight his enemies at length, he prefers to destroy their temple and kill as many of their leaders as possible in the process.

We find a similar lesson in *Gilgamesh*.[21] This warrior himself is

---

21. There was a historical Gilgamesh who reigned over the city of Uruk in Sumer in the third millennium B.C.E.; the poem that survives is dated to at least the beginnings of the second millennium.

"two-thirds a god," and spreads trouble among his subjects by "taking daughters from their fathers and wives from their husbands" (I'm betting nonorgasmically). To remedy the situation, the gods create the hairy Enkidu, who grew up in the desert undisturbed by society and the temptations of the flesh. His power is awesome and he protects the animal kingdom from men. Enkidu fills in the trench-pits of hunters and tears their nets; his strength is equal to that of an army and because of this, no one dares to venture out into the desert.

But Gilgamesh, who has quickly come up with a solution to leave Enkidu without power, proceeds to send a man into the wilderness:

> Go and take with thee a harlot. When he accompanies his flock [of gazelles] to the drinking trough, let her remove her robe. Let him take his pleasure of her.

Once this is done, Enkidu is powerless; upon seeing him in this state, his gazelles flee. He returns to sit at the harlot's feet, where she completes his taming with flattery:

> Thou art beautiful, Enkidu, thou art like a god.
> Why doest thou roam the desert with wild flocks?
> Come! I shall lead you to Erech within the walls. . .[22]

And so, without resistance, Enkidu meekly allows himself to be conducted to the city of Erech, where he becomes semi-civilized.

The goddess Athena shows yet another example of the power of nei kung as practiced by the warrior elite. In the Acropolis museum there is a statue of her defeating a giant in battle (figure 29). Snakes—as we have seen, a symbol of the power of ch'i—fly from her outstretched hands to topple her enemy. Even further, it seems no coincidence that Athena is a virgin goddess, free from the power drain of orgasmic sex.

There is an interesting point to be made in asking why it is that these heroes were deified in ancient Greece, Rome, Egypt, Babylonia,

---

22. *New Larouse Encyclopedia of Mythology* (London: Hamlyn, 1979).

China, and India. One possible answer, viewing the circumstances
through the lens we have set up, is
that in practicing nei kung to gain
power in their earthly life, they
were able to take their yang with
them when they died. I will bring
to your attention once again the
stanza in the *Tao Te Ching*:

> Those who retain their cen-
> ter endure.
> Those who die but continue
> to exist are immortal.

These heroes upon death became potent spirits with power
over the physical world; it is thus

Fig. 29. Athena battling a giant,
from a statue in the Acropolis.
Snakes—representing the power of
ch'i—fly from her arms and hands.

that nei kung was quite possibly the essence and justification behind
hero worship throughout the world in ancient times.

Finally, I would like to combine two Greek words and institute
a new term for the global method of honorable combat typified by
the martial art practiced by these men (and women): *panmachon*
(*pan* meaning "all" and *machi* meaning, as we have seen, "honorable
combat"). Panmachon began in ancient times and marked the development of mankind throughout the Bronze and Classical Ages.
It has reached through time to my master's master, and to John
Chang and to me.[23]

---

23. I have news for the reader who thinks that I am overly ethnocentric in my use of
Greek words: I have been accused in Greece of being an agent of foreign powers for my
supposedly "anti-Greek" stance in many of my writings. Being a Mo-ist, I am preoccupied
with the *essence* of things and rarely with the trappings thereof—*panmachon* defines matters
nicely. In any case, most technical terms in English are derived from the Greek or Latin.
Being Greek, I made the easier choice. No disrespect toward any culture or obfuscation
of history is intended. Besides, there are indications that *panmachon* is the word that the
ancient Greeks used for "martial arts."

Though once multicultural in distribution, it is unquestionable that all martial arts practiced today are either a direct derivation of, or have been heavily influenced by, the martial arts of the Orient. For further information I encourage the studious reader to refer to appendix 1, note 4.

Chapter 7
PRACTICE

"Hey, aren't you Kosta Danaos?" A young man intercepted me on the streets of downtown Athens, stepping directly into my path. I was surprised he knew my face—that was quite rare. He stood directly before me, very sure of himself.

"I'm afraid so," I said. "What can I do for you?"

"Well, I study kickboxing with Mr. X."

"Wonderful—he's a very good teacher. Produced a couple world champions, hasn't he?"

He looked me up and down, sizing me up. He didn't appear impressed.

"I've heard some stories about you and read the stuff you've written."

"Mmm hmmm," I offered. I looked him over—for a moment it seemed as if he were gathering up the courage to attack me. I concentrated my awareness more tightly on the present moment, relaxed my breathing, and locked my senses onto my new acquaintance's movements. I noted my ch'i rising of its own accord, the palms of my hands turning first red then purple, my hands growing heavy and hard. The young man must have felt something—he took two steps back.

"I've been looking for you for two years!" he finally blurted out. "Can you tell me why the hell you don't accept new students?"

"I do accept students," I said, "but I like to get to know them first. Don't you prefer to choose the people you invite into your own house?"

"What's that got to do with it?"

"My students are family to me."

That shocked him completely. I wound up buying him coffee and sat down with him for a couple hours. As it turned out, he had been looking for someone like my master all his life.

Since the publication of *The Magus of Java*, I have been flooded with letters from people demanding either John Chang's true name and address, or, failing that, instruction from any of the members of the Wenwukuan. The truth is that as of this writing, my master has forbidden me to reveal his address and is adamant about not accepting new students. (It is strictly up to him whether or not this will change in the future.)

As for myself, I have always wanted to pass on to the general public what I have learned from John Chang. Indeed, the primary purpose of both this text and *The Magus of Java* is to coerce people to attempt a simple meditative discipline—the first step in a nei kung practice. It is unfortunate that John is oath-bound to teach only his own students, and that I myself am constrained by a similar promise; thus, I cannot spell out for you in detail what you probably most want to know: the specific psychoenergetic practices of the Mo-Pai. Having made the decision to take on students and having accepted the responsibility and karma of this decision, I am allowed to teach these practices only to those I work with in this capacity. As such, I screen people very carefully before consenting to teach them, a process that necessarily results in frustration for some.

In a catch-22 that is typical of such endeavors, when John asked permission from his noncorporeal master to release his story and teachings to the world, the answer was something akin to, "If you can do it in such a way as to get people to meditate, it would be a very wonderful thing; if it backfires, however, or becomes a Frankenstein monster of sorts, you must bear the karma for this result."

In essence, Liao Sigung[1] asked us to get the cart moving, but warned us that if an axle or a wheel broke, we were in trouble. Hence we chose to move carefully and with much forethought. However, we do have the leeway of pushing the envelope. I myself, being a Greek, will walk one step farther and march right onto the line—if there is a court system in the afterlife, a good lawyer should get me off.

Much of what follows in these pages has been approved by John (who really does want everyone and anyone reading this text to begin meditating). Study this book carefully; I have left clues strewn everywhere (and in *The Magus of Java*, as well). If you can piece things together, good for you. Even Liao Sifu would be most happy.

In this chapter, we will talk about the two training regimens basic to Mo-Pai training. In order of importance, these are meditation and standing.

MEDITATION

I am often asked how to meditate. Regrettably, the answer is always the same: I really cannot tell you how to go about it. One of the earliest things I learned from John Chang was that each of us has to find his or her own way into meditation, that there is no general method suitable for all. Through the grace of the universal spirit, we are all individuals—each of us must find an individual path.

Finally, at this time, before launching into the practical aspects of meditation, I'd like to say a word on a common trap of today that I term *materialistic spirituality*. Please do not confuse this term with the designation *spiritual materialism* made famous by the late Chögyam Trungpa.[2] Spiritual materialism refers to a trainee indulging in spirituality as if it were another consumer good, a substitute for material possessions (i.e., "I may be a total blow-out in life, but, boy,

---

1. Sigung means "grandfather-teacher" or "grandmaster."

2. Chögyam Trungpa, *Cutting Through Spiritual Materialism* (Boston: Shambhala, 1987).

am I spiritual!"). This approach leads to nothing. One of Ghandi's greatest lessons was that, in order for one to become a renunciant, he must first have something to renounce.[3] *Materialistic spirituality* refers not to the trainee, but to the teacher—to those who prey like hawks on students who would indulge in spiritual materialism. There are many such vultures around. I am referring to the lamas who sell initiations or who, for a fee, will recognize an individual as a rinpoche; the yogis who charge a thousand dollars to teach a simple meditative exercise; the spiritualists who defraud widows and widowers with electronics and detective work; the Bible-thumping preachers who pass the tray and purchase a new Cadillac; the gurus who use tantra as a means of getting sex. Worst of all are those representatives of the established major five religions who combine spirituality with politics and line their pockets with gold in the name of God. The list is endless, and shames us all.

Materialistic spirituality is one of my pet peeves. It would be an outright lie to claim that I could teach you to meditate through a book. I *do* want to do my part, however, to protect you from the hawks circling above. To reach true meditation, certain standards must be maintained. All I can do here, then, is describe these factors and thereby help you reach the state of meditation.

You Are Your Body

Now, with my warning taken care of, let me begin by defining normal meditation as that state of awareness between waking and sleeping corresponding to the theta waves of consciousness. A powerful meditator can enter into the delta state as well—and beyond, on occasion. A true immortal, like my master, can enter into a state of suspended animation wherein he will not need to draw a breath for eight continuous days.

---

3. This great yogi and statesman was a successful lawyer before giving up his practice to pursue other things.

I myself have had only three experiences to date with a lesser state of suspended animation, and have never exceeded fifteen minutes of stillness. During this time interval, I did not draw a breath, and I cannot with veracity specify the rhythm of my heartbeat. What I can say is that breath retention is for some reason an initiatory process, that there are specific consistent phenomena that can be observed (sights and sounds, though I doubt that the sensory organs themselves play a role), and that the sensation is pleasant once your initial fear is overcome.

But I should hardly write about phenomena that I myself am only now beginning to experience. Instead, let's concentrate on the simple meditation that is our birthright, the process by which we can restore the energies stolen from us by the grind of daily life.

Many authors have expounded on the unity of mind and body. I will adjust this maxim and systematize it a bit differently, using a method common to the Mo-Pai and to the esoteric sword schools of medieval Japan. There are, in fact, *four factors* that affect the outcome of the process of meditation: body (as translated into the meditational stance), emotion, bioenergy (ch'i), and mind.

Before I address each one of these factors specifically, I would like to establish here a very particular perspective on the relationship between you and your body that figures into the practice of meditation. As I have stated earlier, we think with our bodies; there is no way around this. Your personal unconscious is directly tied to the cells of the body that is yours. What I am stating here is a profound diversion from the Judeo-Christian/Cartesian theories that hold sway in Western society, in which the immortal soul resides within the vessel of the body. Nothing could be further from the truth. Your soul is *not* something independent of your body any more than your heart is independent of its circulatory system; in essence, *you are your body*. Every thought you make has a concomitant neurophysiological reaction associated with it, which in our day and age can be observed and possibly even measured. In time (if they do not exist already in the service of our governments), machines will appear that can read minds or broadcast thoughts into minds—and this process will be based on chemistry and electromagnetics, not sorcery.

A chemical introduced into the bloodstream can control the process of thought; many patients, prisoners, and drug abusers alike can bear testimony to this. An injury to the brain (or any major organ for that matter) will affect the personality of the victim. These are commonly accepted axioms recognized by all in that they have been clinically proven. Conversely, our thoughts and emotions can affect our body as well. Much ado has been made over psychosomatic illnesses in medical literature, and hypochondria itself has become a common ailment throughout the world. Is it therefore illogical to suggest that this is a reversible process, and that body and soul are one? I will repeat it again: you do not live *in* your body, you *are* your body.

What this maxim means with regard to a meditation practice is that specific meditational stances will bring about specific individual effects.

The Meditational Stance

The first factor affecting the outcome of meditation is the stance assumed for the practice. Should you choose to meditate in the Japanese kneeling stance of *seiza* made popular by *aikido* and *zen*, the neural and mental effect produced will be different from that produced by, say, meditation in the full lotus position. Students of yoga will recognize the yogic doctrine I am paraphrasing.[4] Sadly, I am speaking from personal experience when I say that I, ever the skeptic, had to have these things proved to me repeatedly before I finally recognized them to be true.

The first thing to be concerned with when attempting meditation, then, is the physical stance you assume before beginning.

I do not want to belabor a point that has been thoroughly analyzed in the thousands of volumes written on the subject, but I

---

4. Indeed, much of yoga is based on the prescription of specific stances, or *asanas*, for the individual.

will, for precision's sake, touch lightly on the best stance for meditation according to the lineage of the Mo-Pai, the full lotus. The half-lotus is the next most desirable stance, though it should be noted that the efficiency of the full lotus is almost double that of the half-lotus. If you can assume neither position, then it would be best to simply sit down on the ground and cross your legs in front of you.

It is important that the top of your head is pointing toward the sky and the base of your pelvis is touching the earth. Your spine should be straight, your shoulders relaxed. Place your hands where they are comfortable. In the Mo-Pai tradition, it is best to concentrate on the dantien while attempting meditation. Other schools recommend other points, but it has been the experience of our tradition that the dantien point is safer and more practical. This assertion has been born out by other Chinese lineages intimately involved with the subject of bioenergy and meditation.[5] Indeed, Chinese hospitals researching the training have clinically documented many cases of insanity caused by the practice of ch'i kung due to the practitioner attempting to move the focal point of his exercise away from the dantien before he was ready to do so. The dantien is like a vast warehouse that will absorb troubles and blessings alike with relative safety.

Your Emotional State

The next factor to consider when meditating is your emotional state. This is much more difficult than it seems. In the martial arts, maintaining an aware and undisturbed mind is of primary importance. This awareness of mind must be maintained throughout any confrontation and beyond (some say in every moment of life). The greatest destroyer of this awareness is emotional imbalance.

The stereotype of the killer with a machine's personality, ice cold

---

5. Chen Xiaowang, private conversation. Grandmaster Chen is the nineteenth-generation standard bearer for the Chen clan, the family to whom all modern lineages of t'ai chi chuan trace their roots.

and indifferent, is not really appropriate to the martial arts, or to meditative practices for that matter. Indeed, our emotions should flow freely and naturally, unfettered by the shackles of the mind. Because our emotions are intimately linked to our personal unconscious mind and thereby to the flow of bioenergy, suppressing those emotions is ludicrous. It is be like placing a bottleneck into a steadily flowing stream—in the long run, there will be problems. We should allow our emotions expression without encumbrance, like a child's. This might mean that you could be completely enraged one minute and smiling and laughing the next. The usual result is that you are quite happy and content much of the time. Of course, people may assume that you are strange, immature, or even crazy—but that is their problem in the end, not yours. It is because of the suppression of emotion imposed by our society that 25 percent of the population in Western nations is taking antidepressants. If you want to truly meditate, your bioenergy must run freely, and that means your emotions must not be shackled.[6]

Allowing your emotions to flow freely results in their automatic prioritization by your central nervous system, which means that they will not impair performance. For example, a few years back I took a spill on my motorcycle; I hit an oil slick while going quite fast around a corner. My martial arts training took over and my body reacted automatically. Everything slowed down—with crystal clarity I remember laying down the bike while making sure my body was well out of the way. *Wow, this is neat*, I thought as I fell. The bike and I slid together for quite a while. After the motorcycle came to a stop, I continued on for ten more yards. The end result was that I suffered a bloody scratch on one knee and the bike needed a new paint job.

After I stood up, the emotions I *should* have been feeling during the incident began coursing through my body. First came anger: *What (bleeping) idiot spilled the (bleep-bleep-bleep) oil here? May the fleas and ticks of ten thousand camels make their home in his loins!*—and so on. Then came

---

6. There are physiological ramifications from this having to do with the limbic system, but I will not get into them here.

fear, the very real fear that is faced during a brush with death. That shook me for minutes. And finally came relief, the heartfelt relief of a man who had survived a crash. I sent a silent prayer to God and thanked Him for my life. Then I picked up my motorcycle and sped on my way. It was as if it had never happened. I only recalled the incident today after searching my memory for a suitable story to illustrate my point.

If the yang ch'i is indeed an initiator of nuclear transmutation, its existence may well explain specific ailments in the body that are emotion-related, such as the kidney, gall, and urinary tract/bladder stones that plague many people. There are indications that even the *shape* of these stones is influenced by the emotion the particular individual is suppressing at the moment.

Ch'i

We have discussed the third factor, ch'i (bioenergy), at length in both this text and in *The Magus of Java*. Allow me to reiterate that bioenergy is intimately linked to the personal unconscious mind and our emotional context. Since most of this book is directly or indirectly involved with the subject of ch'i, the only additional statement to add here is this: *The more ch'i you have, the easier it is to reach true meditation.*

Mind

The fourth factor, mind, has to do with our personal consciousness, our immediate awareness of *me* and *mine*. The essence of *mind* has been distilled in all religions since the dawn of time. For example, in a Greek Orthodox monastery in Crete I found an inscription that, based on stereotypes, should have been more at home in Buddhist Nepal or Tibet than the sunny Mediterranean: "Mind is the Creator of All and the Reason for All Being."[7] Again, if the yang ch'i induces nuclear

7. It is interesting that this inscription dates to the fourteenth century C.E.

transmutation, then the above axiom is true and our reality is indeed shaped by our minds. In referring to mind, however, I am discussing not only our personal consciousness, but also our personal unconsciousness, and, most importantly, the mass unconscious that truly shapes our physical existence. In essence, reality is a *consensus*; it is whatever we unconsciously agree it is among ourselves (much as we have come to a worldwide understanding of what money is). As an interesting aside, I suggest that much of John's power comes from the fact that he has so much yang ch'i gathered in his dantien that he can affect the course of natural law around him, fundamentally overcoming the reality that has been superimposed on our Universe by our mass unconscious mind.

Basic meditation, then, is predominately involved with calming our conscious mind. You have undoubtedly read about the various methods that can be used to diminish the activity of thought in order to reach the theta states of consciousness or even those farther below. (Call it bringing the conscious and unconscious minds closer together, for in the end this is what is happening—enlightenment itself is nothing more than a union of conscious and unconscious minds.) I will not repeat here the standard dictates of these methods—most of them center on breaking into states of pronounced relaxation. There are thousands of volumes in print describing meditative practices—some use mantras and visualization, others do not. (As a point of interest I will say that the Mo-Pai system employs neither mantras nor visualization in its training regimen.) It's crucially important to note that true meditation is neither concentration nor relaxation. We *use* concentration and relaxation to approach meditation, but in essence meditation happens by itself. You could say that concentration and relaxation are the means by which we approach the Infinite and Eternal, and that meditation is the result of the Infinite ever so briefly opening Its gates for our personal awareness. Concentration is *effort*. Relaxation is *action*. Meditation happens by itself—it is a form of surrender. Things are as simple as that.

TYING TOGETHER ALL FOUR FACTORS

Meditation, in the end, is a very personal thing, as personal as making love and therefore largely based on your own belief system. I encourage you to take a meditation course with a teacher that you feel comfortable with. But by all means, *please pursue meditation as a daily discipline*. It will change your life, improve your health, and grant you countless benefits.

Now, let's assume that you know, or are in the process of learning, how to calm your mind. Perhaps a graphic representation (figure 30) would best describe how the body, emotions, ch'i, and mind work together in the process of meditation:

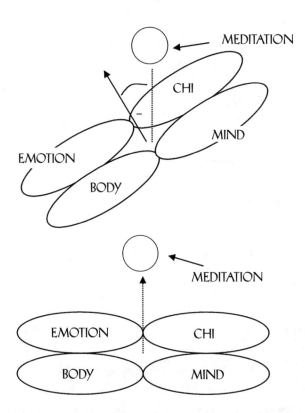

Fig. 30. True meditation cannot be achieved unless the body, emotions, ch'i, and mind are in balance.

In figure 30 you can see that mind, emotion, bioenergy and body lie as circles on one plane, and that above these is a fifth sphere, meditation, which is perpendicular to the plane. In order for true meditation to be achieved, mind, body, emotion, and bioenergy must be in perfect balance.

Let's say that we deviate from that balance toward one particular factor, perhaps emotion (because we are angry with someone) or body (because we have become tired). Preliminary meditation is a sphere; there is some leeway, to enter this state even if your balance slips a little bit. But if the angle of divergence, *theta*, is too pronounced, then you will find yourself outside the sphere and hence outside of meditation. Deeper states of meditation are described by smaller and smaller spheres, which in the end turn into a point from which no deviation is permissible; this point describes *true* meditation. What we can see here is that all four factors are crucial as far as reaching true meditation is concerned.

This does not mean that you need to become Jackie Chan or Krishnamurti in order to engage in meditation; it does mean that you must be in control of your body and allow your emotions to run naturally if you are ever to succeed. It also means that, contrary to expectation, meditation is not strictly a mental process, but is a physical one as well, as corporeal as it is spiritual and cerebral. Treat it as such, and you *will* be successful.

THE PROCESS OF MEDITATION

For tens of thousands of years, people lived in relative harmony with nature and in accord with the world of spirits. Today we admit that aboriginal peoples possess senses that we in our technological grandeur have lost. As recently as twenty years ago, the Khoisan (Bushmen) of South Africa could see the moons of Jupiter with their naked eyes and catch the scent of their prey from miles away. Perhaps, as well, their perception of reality was much more keen than our own, which is why they believed in spirits and communicated with them accordingly and held the belief that our consciousness *does* continue on after death.

John Chang has told me that our spirits are in essence our sub-conscious and unconscious minds, that being dead is the same as dreaming. Our spirits are our yin mind, our physical bodies are our yang mind. By default then, any discipline through which the con-scious, subconscious, and unconscious minds can be brought closer together is of profound benefit to our spirits after death. Meditation is the foremost of these, because it is through meditation that we grow familiar with our true nature. Through meditation we can learn to use the conscious control of our forebrains to calm the raging fears and desires inherent to our limbic system. Through medita-tion, then, we can make our subconscious minds more human, more a part of our true selves, more the consciousness and personality we would like to be.

A Simple Meditation

Following is a simple practice of meditation that can be easily incor-porated into your daily routine.

1. Sit comfortably in a place where you feel "good." You can create such a place inside your home by setting aside a spot and keeping it clean. It is better, however, to meditate in nature, if you can. A backyard is fine.

2. Wear loose clothing. Try to take a shower before you medi-tate. Begin with ten minutes a day and work up to forty-five minutes. Early morning or late at night are the best times to practice.

3. Sit comfortably on the ground or floor. Stretch to the right and left your lower back, spine, and neck in a relaxed man-ner, as shown below (figure 31). Do not force yourself to exceed the natural limits of your body. Simply work gently to make your back, spine, and neck more limber.

Fig. 31

4. Keep your back straight and tuck in your chin. Relax your shoulders and concentrate on your dantien (figure 32).You can follow your breathing, if you wish, or use some kind of visual image or mantra to increase your concentration—whatever works for you. Let the thoughts and problems of the day slip from your mind naturally—don't hang on to them; they will be there when you finish! In time, they will readily leave you of their own accord during meditation. Whenever

your mind wanders, bring it gently back to your dantien. Remember, concentration is effort, relaxation is action. Meditation is to surrender to the Infinite inside ourselves.

Fig. 32

5. While meditating *don't* worry about the act of meditating itself. *Don't* try to establish beforehand how it will feel. *Don't* think about images you will see or may see or books you have read about the practice. There is a way to ensure this: *don't talk about your meditation with your friends.* Keep it private. If you are discussing with others your experiences in meditation, you are in essence calling attention to yourself, and are therefore cheating yourself. Don't do it! Keep it real. Keep it personal.

Circulating the Ch'i—"Standing" Exercises

We have discussed the two circulatory systems for bioenergy inherent in the human body. The exterior system is defined by the points and meridians made popular by acupuncture and is vital for our health and well being. The two largest vessels of ch'i in this exterior system are in the legs, and it is in these extremities that any ch'i not used in our everyday endeavors is stored. In attempting standing exercises then, our goal is twofold: First, we want the ch'i reservoirs in the legs (and the leg muscles themselves) to become stronger, and second, we want that energy to flow up and circulate in the upper body.

The first thing that Liao Sifu taught John Chang was to stand in Ma Bu, the horse stance popularized by the Chinese martial arts today. At first he thought this practice was simply to test or torture him, but in time John realized the benefits of standing—the primary one being that of circulating the ch'i. T'ai chi chuan affects pretty much the same training regimen today—standing in Ma Bu while allowing the ch'i to circulate throughout the body is the basic premise of the exercise known as Standing Pole. For example, in the Mo-Pai system, if a student were to practice only Level-One seated meditation without engaging in a method of balancing out the ch'i, the yang ch'i would eventually gather together and harden in the lower belly of its own accord, effectively preventing the practitioner from advancing any farther than Level One. Thus, circulating the ch'i throughout the body is just as important as gathering it in the first place. In addition to training in standing, practicing t'ai chi chuan with a good teacher from a proper lineage will also aid in circulating bioenergy, and has proved to have outstanding health benefits.

There are many ways to attempt standing. T'ai chi chuan has made many methods popular—there are many excellent books on t'ai chi written by people more qualified than I, and the Standing Pole exercise is covered in them. However, the simplest method of circulating bioenergy, one that John specifically asked me to show for older people or those generally out of shape or with limited leg mobility, does not involve standing at all, but rather sitting in an upright manner (figure 33). This is an exercise that anyone can do anywhere, at anytime—even in the office—and, in conjunction with seated meditation, it will offer countless benefits to the practitioner.

1. Wear loose clothing.
2. Find a chair that fits your body and has armrests. Your el-

bows and knees must be at a 90-degree angle to the floor when you are sitting down with your back straight.

Fig. 33

3. Find a spot where you feel comfortable. A backyard or garden is fine. Even a balcony is fine, if you feel "good" there and the air is clean. If you live in a big city, try to sit in a spot where there are plants and greenery.

4. Sit in the chair, keeping your arms bent at 90 degrees, palms facing the ground. Your back should be straight, your chin tucked in. Do not lean back; your back should not touch the chair. Your legs should be bent at 90 degrees. Keep your mouth closed with your tongue touching the roof of your mouth. Breathe through your nose.

5. Relax your shoulders and concentrate on your dantien. Do not let your back slump—keep it straight. You can follow your breathing, if you wish, or use some kind of visual image or mantra to increase your concentration—whatever works

for you. Let the thoughts and problems of the day slip from your mind naturally—don't hang on to them, just keep concentrating on your dantien. In time, your body will become warm, and possibly hot. You will lose track of time. Do not be alarmed—this is normal.

6. Begin with ten minutes a day and work yourself up to half an hour or more.

7. If you are physically fit, you can use the same technique to circulate energy while standing in the horse stance, Ma Bu, as shown (figure 34). Standing as in t'ai chi chuan is the best for someone in average physical condition (figure 34a). If you have high blood pressure but are otherwise in shape, stand as shown, with your palms pointing toward the ground or floor (figure 34b). For athletes and regular meditators only, because the ch'i is kept inside the lower body, use the stance practiced by John Chang as a child (figure 34c).

(a)   (b)   (c)

Fig. 34

Ancient cultures called the spirits of the dead *shades,* and this word's meaning is quite literal—most spirits are little more than the shadows of the people they once were. Engaging in meditation while we're alive helps us to avoid the risk, when the time comes to die, that our enduring consciousness, our soul, will become nothing more than an assimilation of our fears, desires, and basic memories, a mockery of our personality, a simulacrum of what we once were. Meditation can keep us from becoming a shade in death, rather than the spirit of a true person.

All ancient belief systems (before they became the institutions—religions—that they are today) believed in personal catharsis, a journey we all had to make through our own means. We cannot allow others to carry us, tempting as it may be (though it is true we may be *aided* by others). Meditation is one of the last true tools to survive the millennia unscathed, perhaps because it has been the most difficult to distinguish and persecute. When the time comes to pass on, you cannot take your Rolex with you, nor will you ride in your Mercedes or Lexus. All we take with us is the sum of our thoughts, our memories, and our strongest feelings, good and bad; this will lead us on to wherever we are destined to go. Meditation is a method of cleansing our innermost self, a preparation for what must inevitably come. Please, then, do engage in this discipline in whatever way suits you best. May the words in this text inspire you, and may my own plea guide you.

Chapter 8
WENWUKUAN STORIES

The following short stories are included simply to further illustrate points already made in the text. They are true narratives, the experiences of myself, my friends, and my students. I hope you enjoy them.

THE SAINT

Axiom number one: *We create things in our own image.*

The Greek Orthodox Church is a theocratic institution with a seventeen-hundred-year-old history. For this reason, if no other, I adored it as a child and harbored a strong resentment against it as an adolescent. As a devotee of Eastern thought and a writer who does not hesitate to voice his opinions, I have often been the target of persecution by the religious authority in Greece. This is not something I have sought out for myself, but rather a suppression that has followed me around simply because I have dared to research spiritual belief in general.

As an outspoken martial artist, I am right up there on the Church's blacklist. But I am more a thorn in the heel than an enemy to be stomped on, for two distinct reasons. The first is that I am nominally

138

an Orthodox Christian myself,[1] and while I question dogma, as any educated man of diverse experience will, I have never written against the essence of Christianity (nor do I have any reason to).[2] The second is that I keep a low profile, and while my name is known, my face is not—this gives me considerable freedom of movement, and allows me to approach whom I will.

Some time ago, I was visiting the *sanctum sanctorum* of Orthodox Christianity, the monastic community of Mt. Athos, in search of a saint. The monastic complexes on that rocky peninsula are about a thousand years old, but people had sought solitude there long before communal institutions were organized. Prior to the arrival of Christianity the promontory was sacred to the goddess Aphrodite. I had not yet met my own master and had heard much about a given monk by the name of Paisios residing nearby, reputably a great healer and mystic. (He was later posthumously canonized as Osios, or Almost a Saint; I remember laughing, wondering how such a thing as sainthood could be measured.)

I found Paisios immediately; he resided in a small hermitage not far from the monastery of Koutloumousi. He was from a village near my own—because of this I had procured a letter of introduction to him from a relative. Father Paisios made me most welcome and offered me sweets and water. After exchanging a few pleasantries, we got down to business.

---

1. Orthodox Christianity was bloodily and brutally imposed on the Greeks by their Roman conquerors, but in the end, through Neoplatonism, absorbed many elements of ancient Greek philosophy and culture. It has also still managed to retain as its central dogma the love of God for man. It is for these reasons that I remain, nominally, an Orthodox Christian.
2. This is what got Nikos Kazantzakis, renowned author of *Zorba the Greek* and *The Last Temptation of Christ*, excommunicated. Because the church legally owns all burial plots in Greece, Kazantzakis was buried on private property, for the priesthood did not allow his body to lie in hallowed ground. Today thousands make the pilgrimage to his grave every year, where the following words are engraved: *I fear nothing, I hope for nothing, I am free.*

"How can I help you?" he asked.

I took a deep breath. It was going to be long speech, and I had about a billion questions. What was the nature of God? How should He be approached? What was the nature of man? And what of this nonsense about the Garden of Eden—I mean, it's all metaphorical, right? How do you accept this and that and what is your opinion about this and . . .?

He cut me off—almost hurriedly, with an amused expression on his face—before the first word was out of my mouth. In fact, he spoke so suddenly that my mouth gaped open.

"In my opinion," he said, "it all comes down to prayer and the grace of God. This is what I have discovered in a lifetime of solitude. The key to liberation is prayer; we are not capable of ascending to God through our own efforts, but must ask God to reveal himself to us. When we are clean enough inside, he does so."

I was silent. I did not agree with this conclusion, but he had answered my questions—all of them—before I managed to utter a single word.

"I have a lot to do today," he finished as he stood. "Don't worry, son; you will find your Way very soon."

It was one month later that I went to Indonesia and found John Chang.

After that gentle but curt dismissal, I spent about a week in Athos, roaming around the monasteries in search of other enlightened individuals. The truth be told, I found nothing but fanaticism and dogma there, but the experience was wonderful nonetheless, simply because the historic treasures hoarded in such monasteries are a sight to behold.

Some time after my visit with Paisios I met Kyriakos at the monastery of Agia Lavra.

Kyriakos was a junky—heroin was a habit that had ruined his life and he had gone to Athos searching for solace. I had never been around someone with such a fixation, and while my first inclination was to shy away from the man, in time I found that I actually liked him. He was well educated, had traveled much, and made for interesting conversation. Kyriakos had studied art in Florence—he was a wonderful painter whose talent had been ravaged by the monkey on his back.

It turned out that we were heading back to civilization on the same day. It was a six-hour walk, a beautiful morning, and while we walked it came out that Kyriakos had never met Paisios.

"Well," I said, "if we pick up the pace, we'd still have time to spend an hour with him before the boat leaves for Ouranoupoli."[3]

I proceeded to drag the grumbling and complaining Kyriakos on a forced march, all the while listening to comments about fascists and macho martial artists harboring sadomasochistic manias, and about many other things much less polite. We made the six-hour walk in five hours, though, and, accordingly, had plenty of time to visit Osios.

He was happy to see me. "What are you doing back here?" he asked.

"I just wanted to see you again," I answered.

"Ah. Well, you've seen me again. It will be the last time."

I was shocked by his words, construing that they were meant to be offensive. But Paisios was simply saying good-bye in his innately gruff manner; he was to die of cancer in less than a year and probably knew it. I never saw him again.

He turned his eyes on Kyriakos; they seemed to glow.

"Where are you from, son?" he asked him.

"From Athens," Kyriakos answered.

"You're an artist, right?"

We were both shocked. How did he know? How *could* he know?

"Yes, Father."

"What do you draw?"

Kyriakos threw down his backpack and started rummaging through it, pulling out a sheaf of sketches to show the monk.

---

3. Ouranoupoli is a small town on the Athos peninsula and the laity's entrance point onto The Holy Mountain, which, like the Vatican, is a self-governing theocratic state.

"Um . . . well, here on Athos I've drawn the monasteries, the monks, the mountains . . ."

The dark eyes never left him.

"You draw *yourself*, son," Paisios told him. "Fix yourself first, and then you can become a true artist."

Kyriakos broke into sobs. This was no simple buried emotion coming through—they bubbled up from his *heart*.

Paisios pulled him over to a corner and spent about fifteen minutes listening to his confession. When they finished, Kyriakos's T-shirt was drenched with tears, but his eyes were shining.

We bid the old monk good-bye, scurrying to catch the boat before it left. Kyriakos ran along the path ahead of me. "Come on, you grouch," he shouted back at me. "Hurry up!" Whatever the old monk had done to him had enhanced his physical powers as well as his sense of himself and the world.

It was the first—and to date the only—time in my life that I have seen the central doctrine of Christianity actually applied; that is, the forgiving of sins in the name of God. Paisios's blessing had been no empty ritual. The old monk had given the young addict absolution and that benediction had held true, reaching into the realm of the physical. Kyriakos was a changed man; the monkey was off his back.

You draw yourself, son, the old priest had told him. *Fix yourself first, and then you can become a true artist.* It was then that I realized that all things we create are in our own image, and that this holds true for our view of all aspects of our world.

RESURRECTION

Axiom number two: *We are born into the world naked and exit the world naked as well.*

Bobby had been dead for seven days, but sprang back to life on the day of his funeral. His story is the parable I use whenever I try to convince people to attempt meditation. I would like to share it here with you in hopes that you, too, will learn from it. Like all stories and anecdotes in this text, it's true, and anyone with enough perseverance could probably meet the man and verify the story for himself.

I was quite familiar with his story when we gathered in a luxury hotel in urban Java to discuss a potential business transaction with Bobby's boss. Bobby is fluent in both English and Mandarin, and so was an unparalleled translator for both sides. However, we were both junior adjutants for the group—as is the custom in the Orient, after a time the older men stepped in and started discussing things among themselves. This left me alone with Bobby for the first time since I had met him. I could not hide my eagerness. *What the hell*, I thought, *this guy is as Western as he is Chinese*. Making sure that the proper etiquette was observed (but just barely), I pulled him over to a corner.

"You know," I said, "I've heard your story from others but never firsthand from you. I'd like to use it in one of my books."

He was an incredibly poised, content, and well-groomed man. "All right, he laughed, "I hope that people will learn from it."

We sat down—close enough to the other men so that they could call us, if need be, but far enough away to have a private conversation.

"I was a Singapore policeman," he began, "trained in negotiation. Singapore does not have much of a crime problem—but we do get desperate people engaging in desperate acts from time to time, so there is always somebody with my type of training on call at all times.

"The day before I died, I happened to pass by the Buddhist temple of Kuan-Yin in the center of Singapore. There was no real reason for the visit. I was not a devout Buddhist at the time; in fact I hardly had any religious feelings at all. Like many people, spirituality for me was a formality; one went to church for weddings and funerals. But that day, for some reason, I wanted to light up an incense stick and pray. I don't know why, maybe I had a premonition. The head priestess, as soon as she saw me, called me over to one side. She had seen my fate, she said, and told me that I was in grave danger. I had a dark spot floating over my head, she said. I was to stay at home for all of the following day and the day after.

"The next morning I called my supervisor at work and told him I wasn't feeling very well, that I couldn't come in that day. I told him about my meeting with the priestess as well. It was the holiday season, however, and all my replacements were on leave. I was the only negotiator in the district. 'Come on,' he told me, 'this is Singapore, the safest place in the world. What can happen to you in Singapore? Sit in the back room and sleep all day if you are not feeling well.' He managed to convince me and I went in to work.

"The day passed quietly. That night, however, I got a call from the dispatcher. There was a woman on a bridge over a highway, attempting suicide. They needed a negotiator to talk her down. So I went.

"We parked our police car by the railing, lights flashing, and I did manage to eventually talk her off that bridge. She came down and stood with us by the side of the road, but because in Singapore everything is governed by regulations, I could not let her get into the cruiser until she had been searched and only a female officer could search her. So we stood on the side of the road, waiting for a female police officer to arrive.

"I never saw the car that hit me but I did somehow feel it. I pushed my partner and the woman over the railing into the dead zone between lanes. Then everything went black; I felt nothing, no pain. I was told later that a van hit me—I was driven through its windscreen into the passenger compartment, then the van fell onto the cruiser. It was a mess.

"Like I said, I felt nothing. I woke up to find people swarming all over the accident scene. I tried to talk to them but no one would answer me. I saw my partner and the woman standing there and thought, *Good, I managed to save them*. Then suddenly I was bathed in light.

"Five colors came to greet me. They were incredibly bright, but somehow you could look at them without pain. Yellow, green, blue, red, and white, they all shone down on me. Then without warning, I was in the real Light. It's white but cannot really be labeled with a color. Call it bright. It is bright beyond the sun, but that brightness does not hurt your eyes. All I knew was that I wanted to go into that light. And I realized that this light was not somewhere outside myself, but rather within my own heart. It resides within all our hearts; the light connects us all.[4]

"There were many people standing in the light with me, going into it one by one. They were all naked. I looked down at myself and saw that I was naked too. There were several really beautiful girls around me, but I had no interest in them. I had what felt like a child's innocence; it was then that I knew I had died. I realized that we are born into the world naked and exit the world naked as well; we take nothing with us but our innermost thoughts and feelings in the end.

"I was ready to go into the light myself when suddenly Huang-Ti, the holy emperor of the Chinese people, appeared before me and told me that it was not my time yet, that I had to go back. I don't know if it was really Huang-Ti or a spirit that had taken his shape to make me feel more comfortable and to get my attention. He told me many things then that I am not at liberty to discuss. He stroked my hair and said he would be waiting for me later.

"Then I was back on earth. I could not move. I realized with a start that I was inside a coffin!

"I could only move one hand, so I began to bang on the coffin's lid again and again. After a time, I heard a little girl's voice. I tried to shout but only a strange noise came out. Somebody screamed. The lid was opened and I saw people staring at me.

"I found out later that I was on my way to be burned; they had

---

4. See chapter 4. In addition, it is interesting to note that the Hesychast meditational movement developed by Eastern Orthodox Christianity, which seeks the Uncreated Light, concentrates on the heart and "sealing the breath" in that area—essentially "piercing" the heart chakra. (Please see also appendix 1, note 5.)

opened the coffin thirty minutes before my cremation. What had saved me was the Chinese custom of waiting for one week before burning the dead. My niece heard me banging on the coffin; at first she was afraid of me—she thought I was a ghost—but then she tried to talk to me. Her bravery saved my life.

"I was taken to a hospital. Both my legs were broken, and one arm. My face was a mess and I had lost an eye; seventeen operations later my looks are almost back to normal. And amazingly, I received a present from the Beyond: I spoke fluent Mandarin Chinese, whereas before my accident I spoke only English! This was a gift from Huang-Ti, I think. It is to him that I owe my current occupation as a translator.

"And do you know what is the truly astonishing part of the story? Remember the head priestess at the temple? Well, she disappeared the night of my accident. After seven days, the day of my funeral, they opened the locked door to her room and found her. She had been dead for seven days! They also found a letter from her to me. Writing that letter was the last thing she did.

"I think she chose to die in my place," Bobby concluded, "taking my karma onto herself. I hope to be able to repay her kindness, in this life or the next. But you know what?" He smiled. "What I want more than anything else is to be able to go back into that light again."

"Bobbie, that's one hell of a story." I was choked up. "You must share it with anyone and everyone you can."

Then he smiled conspiratorially, "I died again, for a second time, but on that occasion for only two days."

"You're kidding. . . ."

He began to tell me more, but suddenly we were called to the table where a discussion of the merits and deficiencies of one type of computer software over another suddenly took the place of our discussion of metaphysics. We had stepped back from the forgotten side of ourselves into our modern and equally pertinent reality. Since that day, I have not yet had a chance to hear the rest of his story

But I will. There is no question that I will.

TALKING WITH DAD

Axiom number three: *Speaking with a spirit is as natural a process as taking a nap.*

When my student Stamatis's father died, he and his sister had a series of experiences that bordered on the paranormal. He wrote them down for me and rather than intrude on his version, I have simply translated the text, including it here in his own words.

"I was in Bali with my wife, on vacation, when I was awakened in the middle of the night by a bad dream.

"I dreamed I was back in my parents' house, in my father's bedroom, when I saw my uncle, who had died a year earlier, holding a coffin in his arms. He set it down and I opened it to see my father lying inside. My father moved his arms, though, and I could see he was not dead, so I told my uncle to help me pick him up and lay him on the bed. I then told my uncle to take the coffin away, because I did not want to frighten my father. My uncle did so, leaving the room. Then my father opened his eyes and looked at me.

"'What do you want, Dad?' I asked him.

"'I need to rest, son,' he said. 'I need to sleep and rest.'

"My father had been sick for years, and was quite old. He had suffered repeated heart problems as well as pneumonia, and had been on oxygen twenty-four hours a day during the past month.

"'All right, Dad,' I said, 'we won't bother you. Go ahead and rest.'

"I woke with a start and jumped out of bed, knowing that something had happened to my father—I knew that he had died while I was far away, even though a part of me did not want to believe it.

"I awakened my wife and told her that we had to call Greece to find out what had happened. It was three in the morning. When I finally managed to get through, I learned from my sister that my father had indeed died that evening.

"We returned home in time for the funeral. I had just finished Level One myself, Chang Sigung having determined that I passed the test for this, and was being awakened to a new world of perception. Sifu Chang had told me that my upper centers were being awakened—in fact, while visiting the monastery of Saint Ephraim with Kosta Sifu earlier, I had felt a distinct pressure between my eyes and on the back of my neck when the saint's consciousness had reached out to Kosta. I was familiar with the feeling and was learning to use it. As a result, I could feel my father's presence around our house. It is not something I can put into words; the pressure I described told me that a spirit was present and my heart told me that it was my father.

"One evening, I sat down to meditate inside my own home when I was struck by the scent of flowers, even though we had no flowers in the house. This went on for almost an hour, again and again. My sister Popi had an even stranger experience. She sat down to meditate and felt a tickling sensation on her back. When she stripped later to take a shower, she saw writing on her skin, a fact that was verified by her husband, though the letters could not be made into words.[5] When she told me about this incident, I told her of my experience with the continuous scent of flowers; it turned out that everyone in the family had something to say—a vase had turned over unexpectedly, coffee cups had been breaking of their own accord, and so forth. We decided to tell Kosta.

"My teacher told me that my father's spirit would walk the earth for forty days before he 'went up,' and that this was a normal process. The spirit probably wanted simply to say good-bye, Kosta said; it took a while for them to get used to the transition. He agreed to try and summon my father's spirit with the help of a keris, a bladed weapon of Java that is a powerful talisman.[6] We gathered at the Wenwukuan training hall—my sister Popi, my wife, and I.

---

5. Popi says the marks were primarily *i*'s and *v*'s. We have no idea what the spirit was trying to say.

6. See *The Magus of Java* for a description of the keris.

"Kosta began speaking to the keris, something that set all the dogs in the neighborhood to barking. My wife was startled, but Kosta simply laughed; he told her it happened that way all the time.[7] The dogs quickly went quiet—he continued to ask the keris to search for my father's spirit, that it was imperative we speak to him and tell him that he was frightening his children.

"Suddenly it seemed as if something was going to happen. The air became thick, metallic, and quiet, like the calm before a storm. There were a pressure and a vibration we could all feel.

"Then—nothing. It was if a rubber band had been stretched to its limit and then loosened. Suddenly everything was back to normal.

"Kosta was surprised and troubled; I could see he had been expecting more. He told us that he would telephone John Sigung the next morning to ask for advice.

"In the car on the way back home, Popi admitted to me that she had been terrified. For her participating in such a séance bordered on the practice of magic, something that is strictly forbidden by our Church. She worried that she was committing a sin. I thought perhaps that my father's spirit had sensed her dread, and had not appeared to avoid frightening her.[8] Greece is not Indonesia; we are not used to such cordiality with our dead, and for many conservative Eastern Orthodox Christians in our country today, participating in a séance is clearly considered a sin, an example of black magic. But it was not always that way. In our villages and small towns people still speak of seeing neighbors or relatives in their dreams following their passing.

"Kosta came back with good news from Sifu John: Popi was to fast for a week and, during meditation, ask the spirit to come to her in dreams. This was something that was acceptable in our society.

---

7. Please note: "all the time" being the three times I have attempted this.

8. I myself think the reason is more mundane. The students had not cleaned the training hall for weeks and it stunk to high heaven of sweat and grime. If I were a spirit, I would have stayed away too!

"She did as she was told and indeed, seven days later, my father, holding a bottle of wine, appeared to her in a dream.

"'Father,' she said, 'how are you? Are you okay where you are now?'

"'I'm fine,' he answered. 'This place is great, don't you worry about me.' He gave her a big smile.

"'And you've been drinking, I see,' Popi told him.

"'Well,' he grinned, 'in this place I can drink all I want.' He took a healthy sip of wine in front of her. His deteriorating health had forbidden him to drink alcohol for years while he was alive, and he had missed it greatly.

"Popi wanted to speak with him some more, to ask him if he wanted or needed anything, but because she saw him standing there, well and healthy after he had been sick for years, she felt an uncontrollable urge to hug him. As she proceeded to do so, she remembered he was dead and felt fear, and with that emotion, she awoke.

"Popi fasted for two more days, waiting for my father to try and reach her again, but nothing happened, and she stopped attempting contact.

"I was frustrated; I knew he was around and I wanted to be able to speak with him.

"One day later that week, while I was visiting my mother, I went into my father's bedroom and saw the offerings my family had, by tradition, left out for his spirit. There was an empty glass that had held water which had since evaporated; a crust of bread, which had gone stale; and flowers, which had wilted because of the heat. I refilled the glass, cut him new bread, and filled the vase with fresh basil, which he adored while alive. Then I spoke to him in a low voice, so that my mother could not hear.

"'Dad, I know you can hear me. I know you are here, I can feel your presence all around me. We all love you and we're glad that you are well where you are now. I am not afraid of you—if you need anything or want to tell us something, please come to me in a dream, because that is the only way I can speak with you now.'

"I remembered that he had been so proud that I was practicing the Mo-Pai kung fu. 'This training you are doing is a wonderful thing,' he had said. 'Never stop, never give up.'

"'I passed Level One,' I told his photo. 'I'm training like you wanted. I'll never give up. I'll never stop, just like I promised you.'

"That same night he came to me in a dream. We were at a wedding feast, surrounded by friends, some of whom are still living and some who died some time ago. After spending time together eating, drinking, and gossiping, my father suddenly stood up.

"'It's time for me to go,' he said. 'But I can't find the keys to the door. Can you help me?'

"'Sure Dad,' I said. 'I've got them right here.' Suddenly we were back in the courtyard of our family home, in front of the outer door. I stepped forward and made as if I was unlocking it. The door opened, and my father stepped into the opening.

"'Well, goodness,' he said. 'And here I thought it was locked. Why there's nothing to it!' He passed through the door and was gone, and I awoke suddenly. The clock said it was four in the morning.

"Two days later, in passing by my parent's house again to see my mother, I felt his presence once more. I told him to come and see me if there was anything he had forgotten. That night I saw him again in a dream.

"This time we were at a wake. We stepped out from the church into a large cemetery, where I saw that there was one grave open, perpendicular to the rest. My father pointed to it.

"'Look at that grave,' he said.

"'What is it, Dad? What's wrong?'

"'For us, nothing. Our family is fine,' he said grimly. 'But look at that grave.'

"I awoke, unable to understand him and too afraid to do as he said. The next day I went to the office to discover that the father of a good friend and co-worker had died suddenly and unexpectedly. I attended his funeral that afternoon, and the grave looked exactly as my father had shown me in the dream.

"I understood that my father's spirit was still hanging around, for whatever reason, and tried to reach him in meditation to tell him that he must move on, that it was unwise to linger. I spent the next night in my parent's home, thinking he would come to me again in a dream, but he did not. Rather, the following morning I sensed that he was gone for good; there was no sign of his presence around me; no pressure, no tingling, no light touch on the back of my neck. He had truly and completely departed, to whatever reward God and karma had in store for him.

"I passed by a church and lit a candle for his spirit. Exactly forty days had passed since he died."

LITTLE GREEN MEN

Axiom number four: *Pride and fear make terrible bedfellows.*

There is a cave on Hymittos mountain, near Athens, in which the Nymphs were worshipped in antiquity (the Nymphs were spiritual entities of wood and water accorded the shape of beautiful women by popular fiction). In this cave the philosopher Archedimos passed his golden years, writing and meditating. Today the visitor can see the glyphs he carved on the wall of the cave, inspired by his solitude and, perhaps, by the entities who roamed around him.

People like me can still feel the same lovely ladies dancing in the vicinity at night, and I routinely go there to offer them incense and flowers. Late one particular evening, as I headed up the trail with my little bag full of offerings, I saw a flickering light playing on the walls of the cave, a glow that gave me pause. There is a grate over the mouth of the cavern, placed there by the Department of Antiquities and locked to keep out vandals who had taken to spray-painting the walls. As I stood outside, I could hear ritualistic pagan music coming from the interior of the cave—flutes playing, drums beating, low voices chanting. The little hairs on the back of my neck stood up—I was afraid, with a thousand and one visions of the Twilight Zone casting shadows through my mind.

Curiosity quickly got the better of fear, however, and I decided to peek inside. The padlock that normally sealed the grid had been removed. Thus, in due time, up went the grate, and in went Kosta, tense and apprehensive. Little fears danced through my psyche, gradually taking the shapes of elves and gnomes and weird little men. To comfort me, the ch'i that I had stored in my dantien rose up to protect me like a hooded cobra. I was afraid. My hands began to burn red and heavy, my eyes turned bright. As I groped my way slowly around a corner, I came to see an apparition hanging there, come to life straight from a B-movie: Seven bearded men in purple togas were playing their flutes and drums and chanting around the carved stalagmite altar in the cave.

My hair must have stood straight up, because I remember my first thoughts running along these lines: *Has there been an interdimensional time warp? Are they spirits? Do they mean me ill? Am I in danger?*

Of its own accord, my ch'i came screaming up high; I was suddenly at full power and thus was very, very dangerous. If they were spirits, I reckoned they could not approach a full field of yang ch'i. But my greatest worry was that I did not know by what rules this game was being played. Perhaps in stepping across the threshold, I was in their power. Fear dominated my thoughts.

Suddenly a hand was placed gently on my shoulder—and then I heard a horrible scream. A man went flying through the air, landing with a sickening thud on the hard rock some six feet away. Apparently I had pushed him away from myself—hard. The music suddenly stopped, and the first feeling that flooded through me was relief, followed by this very malicious thought: *They're human—at least they can be hurt.*

When I turned to see the horrified looks on their pasty white faces, I felt like a complete idiot.[9]

The men stepped back at what must have been a strange sight: me, a tall man in gray outdoor clothing, clutching a backpack in my

---

9. Better described by the seven letter word which begins with an *a*.

hands, and their friend lying on the floor, screaming, six feet away. My mind was still stuck in neutral, refusing to function. There was a long period of silence (except for the noise coming from the man on the floor). Then:

> Kosta (*in Greek*): Uh . . . good evening. I didn't mean to . . . (*turns to look at prone man*) Is your friend all right?
> One of them (*very frightened*): Pouvez vous comprendre ce que je dis?
> Kosta (*in a small voice, now feeling like a complete moron*): Oui, mais mal, je crains.

They turned out to be a bunch of crazy French neopagans who wanted to worship the nymphs in their cave on Hymittos. Since the cavern is an archaeological site, they could not do that, especially at night, when access is strictly forbidden. They thought I was a policeman who had come to arrest them—and I, in turn, thought they were something scary beyond my ken. Fortunately the man I had pushed was just bruised and battered, not seriously hurt (even in my terror I had been gentle, shoving but not striking him). The incident made me feel so ashamed, however, that for a whole week I gave them the full guided tour of all the neat places I know in Athens that are not in the guidebooks. The men had a great time, and we still correspond.

This incident was one of many that taught me the danger of both pride and fear. And while I am not a fearful man, pride is a sin I commit routinely.

THE TASTE OF TEA

Axiom number five: *Arrogance is an expensive luxury.*

The following story was sent to me by Andrew,[10] an American student of the Mo-Pai who has lived in Indonesia for the last ten

---

10. Not Andreas, the Australian student in *The Magus of Java.* Andrew is a Texan.

years. It refers to a gathering of students that occurred in a local coffee shop while we were waiting to make a trip to central Java. Again, I allow Andrew to speak in his own words.

"Two students had come to see their Sifu. Sunil, who had a Ph.D. in engineering, had just finished explaining his ideas about the biochemical and biomagnetic nature of ch'i. The master had listened with interest, nodding occasionally, correcting here and there. I watched from the sidelines, sipping my coffee and listening in.

"As Sunil finished, Kosta entered the room holding a book,[11] which he placed on the table in front of Sifu.

"'Sifu,' he said, 'this is the book I wrote about you. It is very popular now. I bought this in the airport bookstore on my way here.'

"'Oh,' exclaimed Sifu as he looked at the cover.

"Sunil placed his hand on the book and interrupted. 'The problem with this book and with Kosta, Sifu, is that he is too full of himself to really understand what you are teaching. His rational Western mind blocks out the abstract element at the core of your teaching.'

"'What do you mean?' asked Sifu.

"'I will tell you a story, Sifu. This will help you to understand.'

"'A famous academic came to the home of a venerated master of Zen Buddhism. He was accorded the honor and respect to which he had become accustomed and was duly shown to a small room in the center of which the Zen master was seated. The academic spoke first.

"I have come to learn about Zen from you, Master. I have read all the books about it and believe that I have achieved a sufficient level of understanding. Will you tell me whether or not I am correct in this understanding?"
"First let us have some tea," answered the master.
A servant brought in a small table with two cups and a kettle of fragrant tea.
"Please allow me to pour for you," said the master.
He raised the kettle and began to pour tea into his guest's cup.

---

11. *The Magus of Java.*

When the cup was full, he continued to pour and hot tea began to run over onto the table.

"What are you doing, Master? Stop, stop! The cup is already full. There is no room for more."

The master stopped pouring and looked intently at the face of his guest.

"Yes, yes. Now I see. How wonderful" exclaimed the academic. "Unless the cup is empty, there is no room for what you have to teach me. Indeed, I truly understand. Thank you, Master, for showing this to me."

He rose and bowed politely, leaving the room with a smile and a look of wisdom that he had not possessed when he had arrived.

"'You see now, Sifu,' Sunil continued. 'This is like Kosta. He thinks that he knows the secret of your teachings and this blinds him to the possibility of truly understanding. His cup is already full.'

"Sifu smiled and asked, 'Have you ever seen the show *Friends* on television?'

"'Yes, Sifu, I have,' answered Sunil, obviously startled by this unexpected question.

"'I like the place where they gather together to reveal themselves to one another. You know, the coffee shop? Yes, I like that show very much. But another thing I noticed . . .' Sifu continued.

"'What is that?' asked Sunil.

"'They have much bigger cups in the West! Have you seen the coffee mugs they use? They're huge, almost like soup bowls!'

"Kosta stifled a laugh and looked down at his hands to hide his wide grin.

"Sunil sat in stunned silence as Sifu gestured for Kosta to move forward and join them at the table.

"Sifu leaned forward and looked at both his students.

"'The academic left the room not with an understanding of Zen, but with a greater appreciation for his own intellect. He had correctly guessed the master's intention in pouring the tea until it spilled over. He was confident that he had the acknowledgment of such a respected master of Zen.

"'Unfortunately,' remarked Sifu dryly, 'the academic wrote down the account, and it is his story that has clouded the minds of well-intentioned students ever since.

"'Come on now.' John rose suddenly from his chair. 'I'm hungry and I know a great place for *yam cha!*'"

CONCLUSION

There is an old Chinese curse that has become well known: *May you live in interesting times*.

Well, our times have certainly become interesting. As of this writing, I am in my early forties, and despite trying to keep up with things, despite my professional involvement in a high-tech industry, the new millennium is a puzzle to me. It is not *change* that is startling me—change is something that I have grown used to, and have eagerly sought, throughout my life. What is startling are the choices that we are making (or being coerced to make) while in the process of change, the choices that seem to be leading us to devastation.

How is it that a man who speaks so freely of spirits, thunderbolts, and divine intent reflects so disapprovingly on the decisions we as people have been making of late? There are essential elements in our society and our being that should be approached and altered only after careful thought and trial. As Alexander Pope wrote, "Fools rush in where angels fear to tread." In this new millennium, we have lost every sense of security in our lives, the institutions of man having fully replaced nature as our overlord. Money itself, our chosen medium of exchange, has become valueless, an equation in a computer, subject to the whims of the powerful, and to the appetites of traders who seem to think that profit is the only thing that matters in life. Corruption is evident everywhere—what people are getting away with is astonishing to witness. The concepts of justice, fairness, and reciprocity are in decline, replaced by nepotism and networking, ingratitude and ineptitude. Big business does indeed rule, and Big Brother is indeed watching. It seems that our every act and desire is recorded in electronic format, subject to review at any given time by those who feel it is their right to be privy to what has always been considered private. Our food supply has become an abomination—it would be better not to discuss the issue out of respect for my readers' stomachs, but it is surprising that we have even managed to survive, as chemically polluted as food production has become.

In short, greed and ignorance rule our lives, and it is people's unspoken decision to allow them to do so that I, for one, cannot understand. Is it little wonder, then, that the use of both illegal and legal drugs has become epidemic? It is little wonder that our environment is falling to pieces—modern projections estimate that with regard to reversing the process of environmental destruction on earth, we will hit the point of no return within ten years. And then what? Do we hinge our hopes on the peerless powers of modern science to ensure the continuity of our species and our individual survival? Good luck—modern science is far from faultless, a tool to be used, as wise or as stupid as the men who wield it. Many scientists themselves (I among them, if you still wish to call me a scientist) believe that we as a society have once again fallen into the depths. We who have come so far, through so many dark times, have failed and are slipping away, a scant few feet before reaching the final prize.

And yet . . . and yet there is hope. We have stumbled, but we can still pick ourselves up and continue on. There is a chance we may yet pull ourselves to safety from the lip of the black hole we are sliding into. For all our depredation, for all our stupidity, a clean wind is blowing throughout the smog, a glimmer of light through the impending night. People are starting to take a stand. People are beginning to work together for the common good. People are starting to become angry, and it is a righteous anger indeed.

I myself, for one, will not accept the notion that this beautiful home we have been blessed with must inevitably turn into a barren, dog-eat-dog world. Perhaps you will say I am an idealistic anachronism, a throwback to a different era. I would like to think instead that I am ahead of my time. Conceivably, in the future people gazing into the forgotten side of ourselves will have learned to use the implements of modern science in conjunction with the discipline of ages past for the common good. I believe that day will come. It *must* come.

The forgotten side of ourselves, the part of our history that has been discarded, will play a key role in mankind's revival. Hard science will walk hand in hand with psychophysical techniques forged millennia in the past. We will come to understand our true role and true purpose in the universal scheme of things. Can you imagine a world, for example, where a murder is solved not only through modern forensic techniques, but by summoning the spirit of the deceased onto the witness stand through the avenue of government-certified psychics?[1] Can you imagine a world where death has lost its terror, where it is treated as a simple inevitability, a retirement that is planned for, much like growing old? Where the nature of the afterlife itself has been charted and characterized, much the way human anatomy has been? What would it be like to live in such a place? Wouldn't it retain the most valuable commodity sought after today—freedom?

To develop such a world will not be an easy task. We must recall the strategy that bought our survival in primitive times, the tactic through which our greatest achievements have found focus: *synergy*, the joining together of energy toward some common goal. And synergy is a difficult resolution in a world that today proudly proclaims itself dog-eat-dog, where profit and personal pleasure are the principal motivating factors.

---

1. Some of you are thinking, *What a great movie that would make!*

I often ask my students how it is that the Spartans were able to stand at Thermopylae.[2] The answer: *They stood together.* The Greek phalanx of the time was such that each man used his shield to protect not only himself but his neighbor as well—all moved as one with a common purpose. It was the phalanx that made ancient Greece strong, heroic individual combat having been replaced by that time with the armored might of the organized infantry unit. We need to relearn this approach—man is, after all, a pack animal. The only reason we have survived at all is that we once stood together. The forgotten side of ourselves once grew and flowered under the care and mutual support of all men in primal times and within the concept that human beings were an integral part of a greater totality. Perhaps man was more humble back then, awed as he was by the forces he perceived in the Universe. I am sure that we will regain that humility and that perception before it is too late.

Many of my brother students involved in Mo-Pai nei kung train for only themselves (admittedly, quite more fiercely than I do). I say to them and to you, my reader, that such an approach in this modern world is pointless, without merit. It does not matter if only one soul survives a planet that is spiraling into desperation. I myself imagine a world where millions practice nei kung daily, where there is an individual like my master in each city around the globe. It is for this reason that I have written my books, and this hope is indeed why the Wenwukuan was founded.

We must have hope, even as we come to make our final stand. This book began with a dream of dragons, an inexorable link between our forgotten world and our modern one. Let it end there

---

2. I am referring to the well-known story of the three hundred Spartans: In 480 B.C.E., a force of seven thousand men led by the Spartan king Leonidas held the pass at Thermopylae for three days against a Persian army modern estimates place at around 200,000 strong. They were outnumbered by more than twenty to one. While the king and his three-hundred-man bodyguard deserve most of the credit, we cannot ignore the contribution of the other 6,700 men who fought in what has been called The Battle for the West.

as well. Look out your window—the dragons are still there, flying through the bright sky, their scales glistening. Can you hear their thunder? The magic that once quickened our lives, the stories told by grandmothers next to roaring fireplaces . . . that magic still exists. It may be harder to find today, but it is still out there. You never really know when and where you will stumble onto it. For the most, it seeks solitude and lives on in the remote areas left to the world, but it does not necessarily shun the cities of man. My master, John Chang, for example, lives in the heart of urban Java. You can search anywhere for the forgotten side—it could be right next door to you. But you must learn *how* to see, *how* to feel once again, before being able to perceive it.

And then it is yours, no longer forgotten, for as long as you wish it to be. Use it well.

APPENDIX 1

Note 1: Apollonius

Apollonius of Tyana was a great yogi of the Pythagorean school whose biography was recorded by the famous scholar Philostratus at the instruction of the Roman empress Julia Domna. Because this biography portrays a figure much like Christ in power and temperament, it was suppressed by Christian authorities, beginning in the fourth century C.E. and so is virtually unknown today. Indeed, when the work was first translated into English in 1809, the translator, Rev. Edward Berwick, apologized profusely to the Christian world for the similarities the reader was bound to notice between the life of Jesus and that of Apollonius. This controversy is further fueled by the fact that Apollonius's biography was published in 220 C.E.— before the first gospels were canonized.

We cannot in all fairness accept Jesus of Nazareth as an historic figure. Despite the profuse record-keeping of Roman archivists and Jewish scholars alike, not a single verifiable archive has survived of Jesus' life. Apollonius's life is considerably more documented, though a complete account is also lacking. Nevertheless, we can, through indisputable historic records, confirm that Apollonius did indeed exist and that he did do some of the things attributed to him by Philostratus. (The Roman scholar's work may not be accepted as historic documentation, since his main emphasis was to turn Apollonius into a literary figure, rather than to portray the man accurately. Like many authors before and after, Philostratus took many liberties.)

Apollonius was born in the early years of the first century (some say 4 B.C.E., others 1 C.E., still others 40 C.E.) into a prominent family in the Greek town Tyana of Cappadocia, and he traveled extensively throughout the known world. A record of his travels and an account of his life were reportedly kept by his foremost student, Damis. Philostratus later compiled these notes into book form. This account of Apollonius's life is of importance to historians today because, along with the works of Pausanias, it comprises the main literary chronicle we have of the Greek world of that time.

Apollonius is said to have performed the same miracles as Christ: healing the ill and the maimed, exorcising demons and vampires, even raising a little girl from the dead. He refused to call these feats *miracles*, saying that they were simply expressions of natural law.

At the age of fourteen, Apollonius went to the city of Tarsus to study. From Tarsus he went to Aeges, where he was indoctrinated into the Pythagorean school at the age of sixteen. From that time on, he ate no meat, drank no wine, and wore only linen or cotton clothing. In Aeges he also studied at the temple of Aesclepius, where he learned the art of healing. But this was not enough for the young philosopher. Roughly six or seven years later, according to Philostratus, he set off for India to study with the yogis there who, he had heard, were great mystics. On the way he stopped off in Babylon, where he was initiated into the Chaldean mysteries by the magi there. The king of Babylon became his friend and provided him with camels and a guide for his journey.

His next stop was Kashmir to see the ascetics who lived there. He became a student of the sages of Kashmir, learning the inner workings of mind and body and, through this discipline, the mysteries of the Universe itself. After returning to Europe by sea, he became one of the greatest teachers and travelers of all time. Apollonius taught throughout Greece, Italy, and Spain and lived for years in Alexandria and Antioch. He became the personal advisor to prominent Romans and actively involved himself in politics. Like Jesus, he was tried by the Romans, no less than by the emperors

Nero and Domitian. In the first case he was saved by Tingellinus, in the latter he disappeared suddenly from the courtroom, telling Domitian, "You cannot slay me, for I am not mortal." He died around 120 C.E. in deep old age, leaving a profound legacy behind him. The emperor-philosopher Marcus Aurelius, for example, openly admitted that he modeled himself after Apollonius.

Philostratus's *Life of Apollonius of Tyana* first came under attack during the rule of the early Christian emperors. The text was completely suppressed under the direction of the emperor Justinian—who managed to clear the library compiled by Julia Domna of its philosophical "garbage"—and of Pope Gregory in Rome (who was also fond of destroying books he disagreed with). Fortunately, copies of the work managed to survive the pogrom.

Note 2: Mo Tzu

Born in 469 B.C.E. in the state of Lu, roughly ten years after Kung Fu Tzu's passing, Mo Tzu (or Mo Ti) was extremely well educated as a youth and apparently a martial artist and master of strategy as well. Indications are that he was from a poor family and may have even been branded a criminal (Mo Tzu means "Mr. Tattoo"). The principles of justice were the driving force of his ministry, however, and though by nature a stubborn and extreme individual, universality (universal love) was the center of his teaching.[1]

There is some difficulty, however, in using the words *universal love* to describe the central theme of Mo Tzu's philosophy (though the Chinese word *ai* used in the texts does mean love). From my standpoint, the term *universal love* suggests a more Western consciousness than an Eastern approach to life. The reason for my insistence on this distinction is that Mo Ti was preoccupied with justice as much as he was with compassion, and did not tend to be a very forgiving fellow. By contrast, in the West, as a consequence

1. Mo Tzu, Hsun Tzu, and Han Fei Tzu, *The Basic Writings of Mo Tzu, Hsun Tzu, and Han Fei Tzu*, ed. and trans. Burton Watson (New York: Columbia University Press, 1967).

of our Judeo-Christian tradition, universal love has become associated with the forgiveness of sins, which is not really a focus here.[2] Hence my choice of the word *universality* to describe Mo Tzu's teaching, which seems to do a better job of tracing back to the concept of karma. In any case, the universal person considers his neighbor as he does himself and the father of his neighbor as he does his own father, and acts accordingly.

Mo Tzu never hesitated to stand up to the powerful and risked his life on many occasions while doing so. His driving force was a pronounced love for justice. Indeed, Mo Tzu's followers later became the protectors of the common man and of holy places. Heaven is aware of every crime that people commit, he wrote, and heaven loves justice and hates injustice. How does one know that heaven loves justice? In a just world, there is life, wealth, and order, while in an unjust world there is death, poverty, and chaos.

He believed that heaven cherished the entire world universally and sought like benefit for all living beings. According to Mo Tzu, heaven desired that those who have strength protect and work for others, those with wealth share it with others, those in positions of authority work ethically for proper government, while those who labor carry out their tasks diligently. When a state or society as a whole avoids conflict along its borders, feeds the hungry, and ministers to the ill, then that nation will flower and prosper. Almost 2,400 years ago, Mo Tzu wrote that if a country substitutes good government for offensive warfare and spends less on the army, it will gain rich benefits; if a leader acts according to the universal laws of justice and sets an example, then he will have no enemies and bring incalculable benefit to the world. As an example of this, Mo Tzu recounted how many hundreds of officials and how many thousands of soldiers were required for a military expedition. In the meantime internal government would be neglected, farmers would forget their crops,

---

2. The first elder master who inherited the lineage of the Mo-Pai refused to suspend the capital punishment of his son for murder because of his devotion to justice and abhorrence of nepotism.

merchants would hoard their wares. If one-fifth of the supplies and weapons were salvaged afterward, it would be considered fortunate. It was a guarantee that countless men would die or become crippled in a war. Mo Tzu then asked if it was not perverse that the leaders of the world delighted in the injury and extermination of their own citizens.

He actively attacked nepotism as well. Originally, he wrote, government was intended to benefit and help the poor, bring safety where there was danger, and restore order where there was chaos. People chose as leaders the most capable among themselves so that government could be unified under intelligent direction. However, administration in his day was carried out by court flattery, while the relatives and friends of those already in power were exclusively appointed to positions of authority. Since the citizens realized that these individuals had not been commissioned for the welfare of the people, they resented them and did not identify with them, fostering discontent and revolution. Mo Tzu suggested that surely this method of appointment was insane. He suggested that those in positions of power honor the worthy and impartially demote those without ability in the interest of doing away with interpersonal conflicts. It is sad that Mo Tzu's observations are still relevant today; we have learned nothing in two millennia.

Finally, Mo Tzu supported his beliefs in nonhuman spiritual beings and the spirits of human ancestors with evidence that countless people all over the world had experienced encounters with such entities. Overall, his philosophy and worldview from a metaphysical standpoint were very close to the shamanistic model.

For two centuries after his death in 391 B.C.E., the school of Mo Tzu was the main rival to the school of Kung Fu Tzu. His followers, most of whom were from common stock themselves while at the same time being very educated (an unusual combination in the fourth century B.C.E.), became temple guardians and the defenders of the simple man. However, his school quickly broke into three branches, each accusing the other of heresy, and because of this conflict among themselves and with Confucianism, they quickly lost power. By the Common Era they had mostly disappeared or gone underground.

Note 3: Opening a Chakra

What is the difference between opening a chakra and filling a chakra? The first condition is permanent while the second is not.

Let's imagine a vessel made of a particular type of tough plastic gel, and imagine this gel will melt spontaneously when it reaches a specific temperature, thus rendering the receptacle nonexistent. In order for the vessel walls to reach this temperature, however, it has to be heated up with a given amount of energy. This amount of energy is fixed and described by the innate thermal capacity of the container. To make the container melt, we are going to fill it up with a specific amount of hot steam. Under atmospheric pressure, however, the container is unaffected by the fiery gas; in order to cause the melting, we are going to have to place *in compression* the vapor inside the vessel, so that in essence it becomes superheated steam. In summary then, we have three factors to consider: The first is the container, the second is the temperature that it must reach in order to melt, and the third is the amount of superheated steam we must fill the container with so that the necessary temperature can be reached.

Chakras are essentially three- or four-dimensional yin standing waves, as we have said. They possess the capacity to store their opposite, solar yang ch'i, inside the zero nodes of their essence. This capacity is not limitless; we can fill up a chakra to capacity under normal pressure, but can "melt" it when we force the yang energy within it to squeeze together and become "hard."

If a chakra has a given energy level, then the total power required to sever the waves that make up that chakra is defined by the following formula:

$$\text{Power} = {}_0\!\int^t F(E,t)\, d(t)$$

Or: The required power is a given amount of energy (E) accrued over a time (t). The area under the curve is the total power required. At this point the chakra is permanently opened (figure 35).

There is another approach used by many spiritual disciplines. In this case the chakra is "filled" but not "cut." What this means is that

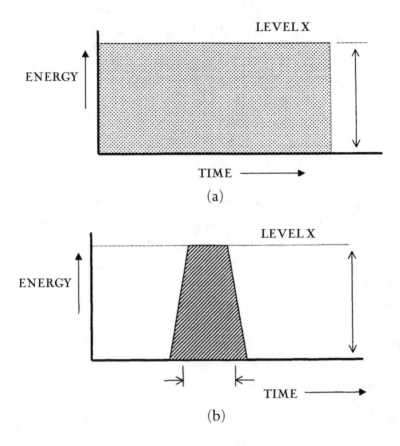

Fig. 35. The energy required to open a chakra permanently (a). The maximum energy inherent in a chakra may be temporarily stored, as shown (b).

for any given length of time, power is placed inside the waveform so that the total energy corresponds to the highest state of the chakra. At this point the adept garners the benefits of the condition (i.e., he develops "powers" or an enhanced awareness), but the condition is not permanent. If the trainee is remiss in his discipline, the yang energy will begin to leach out by osmosis, and he will soon lose all he has achieved. There are yogas (such as the Tibetan *phowa*) that use this approach to enhance awareness during the moment of death, in which case it is perfectly acceptable.

Note 4. Bodhidharma and Chang San Feng

There are essentially two martial traditions in China, Buddhist and Taoist. Popular belief demands that the Buddhist martial arts be tied to the arrival of the Indian sage Bodhidharma at the Shaolin monastery, and the Taoist tradition to Chang San Feng of Wu-Tang mountain. I would like to examine the first thoroughly in a historical context, and touch briefly on the latter.

Most readers have heard the story of Bodhidharma. He was the third son of a king in southern India, a member of the warrior (ksatriya) caste.[3] His Buddhist training took place in Kancipuram, south of Madras, under the direction of the sage Prajnatara, a master of a proto-Mahayana sect. Traditionally, Bodhidharma is thought to have come to the Shaolin temple in Henan province around 520 C.E. and taught the monks there two sets of exercises, the Yijin Ching (sinew-changing scripture) and the Xisui Ching (bone-marrow-washing scripture). (Associations between Buddhism and the Chinese martial arts dating back to the sixth century C.E. have been documented in murals.) It is from these two sets of exercises that Shaolin kung fu is thought to have developed.

But we should more closely examine the legend in order to obtain an understanding of the reality behind it. First of all, we can accurately trace the martial arts in China to the tenth century B.C.E. There are Taoist references to both ch'i kung and nei kung beginning with the *Tao Te Ching*, one more indication that martial, meditational, and bioenergetic disciplines were widespread almost a thousand years before Bodhidharma arrived on the scene. Indeed, there is considerable evidence that there was a Buddhist *dhyana* (Ch'an, Zen) school in China a good two hundred years before his trip to China. Why then does oral tradition demand that he was the founder of kung fu and Ch'an (Zen) Buddhism in general?

---

3. Bodhidharma's story is based on a number of accounts. I would recommend the following as a summary: Michael Maliszewski, *Spiritual Dimensions of the Martial Arts* (Rutland, Vt: Charles E. Tuttle, 1996).

I am convinced this is so because he was a Persian follower of the thunderbolt.

One of the earliest accounts of Bodhidharma[4] refers to him as a "Persian monk" (oral tradition calls him a "blue-eyed Persian"). In our day and age, Iran having become a proponent of Muslim fundamentalism, we have conveniently forgotten the extent of their civilization and the profound debt we owe to Persia; it was the Persians who, between the first and sixth centuries C.E., preserved the wisdom lost to the West with the fanatical institution of Christianity as the state religion by later Roman emperors. Persia and the Bactrian states of the Hindu Kush, having become the crossroads of the world, in essence rescued the learning of the ancient Greek philosophers from the depredations of the new order, and combined it with the wisdom of the East. It is this knowledge that was passed on to the Arabs after their conquest of Persia.

We have discussed the extent of trade in the Bronze Age—but we should not forget that the Silk Road was instituted in the first century B.C.E., and that goods flowed from Luoyang in China to Britain and back on a routine basis. Further, Greek mariners of the age sailed from ports on the Red Sea around India via Indonesia all the way to Canton, trading merchandise! Beginning with Alexander's conquests, the flow of information and goods between Orient and Occident reached phenomenal proportions. Alexander's successors and their descendants penetrated even farther into India, creating kingdoms and becoming the stuff of legends. Some historians say that the list of Greek kings in India is as long as that of the kings of England from the Norman invasion to the present day.[5] The resulting exchange of ideas, information, and artifacts had a profound effect on the history and development of both the East and the West.

We must view Bodhidharma, the thunderbolt, and the history of Buddhism in light of this flow. One has only to look at

---

4. That would be the *Loyang Chile Lan Chi*, written by Yang Hsuan Chin in 547 C.E.
5. George Woodcock, *The Greeks in India* (London: Faber & Faber, Ltd., 1966).

the art and sculpture of the Hindu Kush to realize that a melding of both civilizations and religions had taken place. The kingdom of the Greek king Menander, who became a Buddhist saint, extended in 150 B.C.E. from southern Afghanistan through Rajastan and the Punjab, to reach the Ganges river. Menander filled India with Buddhist stupas. We have already discussed Apollonius of Tyana and his trip to India. If a recent excavation is any indication, there is evidence to suggest that the Roman's had sent a formal ambassador to China. And when, in 353 C.E., the witch hunt against pagan learning was initiated by the newly arisen Christian Roman state, the most popular foreign deities in Greece were the Persian god Mithra and the Egyptian goddess Isis.

Persia then was a pronounced focal point of cultural exchange well into the sixth century C.E. When the Byzantine emperor Justinian shut down the Academy of Plato (in 529 C.E., right around Bodhidharma's time), the Seven Philosophers of Athens sought refuge in Persia. When the Tibetan king Srongtsan Gampo instituted a competition among doctors to determine which medical tradition was superior, it was won by a Persian physician named Galen who practiced Greek medicine (Galen is a Greek name). And recent investigations have shown that the Tibetan folk religion of Bön was introduced in Tibet from Persia via the kingdom of Zhang Zhung.[6] In fact, for a time the entire Near East was a bastion of paganism against the establishment of Christianity. For example, the city of Ba'albek in Lebanon was so militantly idolatrous that St. John Chrysostom sent a task force of monks to destroy the area's temples (roughly 400 C.E.). And around 550 C.E., the emperor Justinian (yes, him again) had to order the destruction of Ba'albek's Temple of the Sun to squelch the rampant paganism in the area. To make sure that the temple was not rebuilt, he carted off its largest pillars to Constantinople, where they were used to support the center arches of his new basilica of Haghia Sophia.[7]

---

6. Two sources: Lopon Tenzin Namdak, *Heart Drops of Dharmakaya* (Ithaca, N.Y.: Snow Lion, 1993); Charles Allen, *The Search for Shangri-La* (London: Abacus, 1999).

7. William Dalrymple, *From the Holy Mountain* (London: Flamingo, 1998).

Now, we have seen that the martial arts were eminently tied to spirituality in the ancient world going back to at least the beginnings of the Bronze Age. The Parthenon, for example, that holiest of places, was decorated with scenes of honorable combat (*machi*), showing unarmed men besting sword-wielding assailants.[8] Indeed, all Greek games were religious festivals celebrating the arts of personal combat, and all athletic competitions were in essence derivatives of the warrior arts. Having said the above, we will now begin to mix speculation with historical documentation in a way that may shed light on some gray areas.

Beginning with Alexander's conquests and continuing throughout the Roman period, the world bore witness to an incredible fusion and diffusion of cultures—in this case, Roman, Greek, Indian, Persian, and Chinese—such as the world has not seen until the present day. For example, in an ancient Egyptian tomb in Alexandria, along with the expected presence of classical Egyptian relics, one finds a pair of very Greek Gorgon's heads below which rise a pair of very Roman bearded serpents wrapped around the caduceus of Hermes. Guarding the entrance to the tomb are the jackal-headed Anubis and the crocodile-headed Sobek, both wearing the armor of Roman legionaries, complete with breastplate, short sword, lance and shield![9,10] If we look farther East, we will find that between 1965 and 1979 a French archaeological mission to Afghanistan turned up an entire Greek city with an estimated population of 50,000 people in the northern part of the country. Ancient literary sources tell us that there were a thousand such Greek cities scattered throughout Afghanistan, Pakistan, and India. But the real miracle occurred after the collapse of the Greek hegemony in 30 B.C.E., when the area was conquered by Parthians and Chinese Kushans. It seems that the Greek population did not leave, but instead stayed on, forging with its presence a new culture.

---

8. Today these murals may be seen in the British Museum.

9. In the British Museum there is a set of Roman armor made entirely from crocodile skin. Perhaps this material was more suitable for warfare in the African desert than metal.

10. Dalrymple, *From the Holy Mountain*.

East met West as never before. The Kushans began using Greek
script for their writing. The Parthians built a temple to Zoroaster
in Taxila that was a replica of the Parthenon in Athens. And when
Buddhism began to spread into the area, religious sculpture was
first undertaken in the Greek manner in Ghandara. It could very
well be that the Mahayana school of Buddhism was derived through
Greek influence.

The importance of the thunderbolt to the Bactrian Greeks can
be seen in the many coins depicting the goddess Athena holding
that weapon. Now, Athena, as we have said, represents culture and
honorable combat and is opposed to Ares, who represents wholesale slaughter and the destruction of civilization. In essence she represents *martial spirituality*. By assigning the thunderbolt to Athena
(while it is normally the prerogative of Zeus alone), the Bactrian
Greeks are giving us a hint as to the primary focus of their warrior
culture. And in the Ghandara sculptures, Buddha's omnipresent
attendant, Vajrapani, is depicted looking very much like the Greek
Zeus. This should come as no surprise, since Vajrapani means quite
simply "thunderbolt in hand," and Zeus was, as we have seen, the
Greek god of thunder, "he who yokes together."[11] Though the evidence is circumstantial, there are altogether too many apparent links
for these elements to be entirely unrelated.

We will return to Ghandara and Buddhism soon, but for now let
us focus once again on Persia. There is one more additional factor
that enters into the soup we are making with this nation as the sea-
soning, and that is the doctrine of Mani.

Manichaeism was a dualistic religious movement founded in Persia
in the third century A.D. by the prophet Mani, who became known as
the Apostle of Light. Mani was born on April 14, 216 C.E., in southern
Babylonia. Before his birth, his father, Patek, a native of Hamadan,

---

11. The main Hindu god of the ksatriya caste was Indra the Thunderer, Hence Zeus
became a substitute through which Hindu doctrine could meet Buddhist without either
side losing face. The resulting potpourri of Buddhist-Hindu-Greek concepts was based
on the common ground uncovered. This amalgamation developed into Mahayana
Buddhism.

had joined a religious sect practicing baptism and abstinence. Through his mother, Mani was related to the Parthian royal family. After his enlightenment at the age of twenty-four, he was given a heavenly order to reveal himself to the world and expound on his teachings. From that point on, Mani preached throughout the Persian Empire and into India proper. For many years unimpeded, he was later persecuted by King Bahram I, who supported Zoroastrianism. After twenty-six days of trials, which his followers called the Passion of the Illuminator, Mani delivered a final message to his disciples and died (sometime between 274 and 277 C.E.).[12]

Mani viewed himself as the final successor in a long line of prophets beginning with Adam and including Buddha, Zoroaster, and Jesus. His religious views followed a similar multiethnic vein—thus he perceived earlier revelations of the truth as being limited in effectiveness, because they were taught in one language to one people. In addition, history had shown him (even back then) that later adherents quickly lost sight of the original truth expounded on by the teacher and developed their own versions. Mani deemed himself the conveyor of a universal message destined to replace all other doctrine worldwide. As such, he recorded his teachings in writing and gave those writings orthodox status during his lifetime.

In essence, both Manichaeism and Mani himself were a product of the internationalism that marked the age; note that this universal doctrine had Persia as its core, for it characterizes that nation as the formal hub of the tremendous cosmopolitan flow that occurred during that period. It should come as no surprise, then, that Manichaeism quickly spread west into the Roman Empire. From Egypt it moved across northern Africa (where St. Augustine for a time became a believer) and reached Rome in the early fourth century. This period marked the height of Manichaean expansion in the West; however, it was soon attacked by both the Christian Church and the Roman state, and so disappeared almost entirely by the end of the sixth century.

12. Encyclopedia Britannica Online, Manichaeism

During the lifetime of Mani, Manichaeism had spread into the eastern territories of the Persian Empire and to India as well. The Manichaean community maintained itself in Persia, in spite of severe persecutions, until the tenth century C.E., when Muslim oppression forced its members into exile.

Mani sought to establish a truly universal religion that would integrate itself into all the partial truths of previous revelations, particularly those of Zoroaster, Buddha, and Jesus. He sought the essence of a truth that could be translated into diverse molds in accordance with the different cultures into which it spread. But at its core, Manichaeism was a type of Gnosticism—a dualistic religion that offered liberation through special knowledge of a spiritual truth. Manichaeism taught that life in this world is fraught with suffering. According to Mani, to know ourselves was to see that our core was directly tied to the very nature of the Absolute—this was enlightenment. Illumination enabled the seeker to understand that, despite his present status in the material world, he did not cease to remain united to the Eternal.

With its preoccupation on the essence of things, its flexibility as far as ritual and dogma were concerned, and its emphasis on inner illumination, it is not too much of a step to theorize that Manichaeism could have influenced the young Bodhidharma and led to the development of Ch'an. As we have seen, Bodhidharma's own teacher was a proponent of the Sarvastivada proto-Mahayana sect—Buddhism itself was well on its way to becoming Hinduized and Hellenized by that time, an outcome of the same pronounced cultural melding (it's easier to worship an anthropomorphic God than to concentrate on an abstract).

Let me propose a theory for which I have only a gut feeling: Bodhidharma's family were Manichaeans; possibly, he was of mixed Persian and Indian extraction. It seems that he was indeed of the ksatriya caste and lived during that time when the Huns were raiding India. As such, he probably grew up practicing the martial art of *vajramukti* from the moment he could walk. I believe that the Greeks, in becoming Buddhists and retaining machi as an integral component of their culture, reaffirmed the Indian ksatriya tradition of combining martial arts with spirituality, and nurtured it into Mahayana Buddhism as that dogma developed. Keeping in mind the profound diffusion of culture during the time, this is not a hard pill to swallow. And in any case, it was no large step, as Shakyamuni Buddha himself was a ksatriya. The tenet of martial spirituality endured for centuries after the Greeks lost power and became the subjects of Parthian, Kushan, and Indian kings. It was this approach that Bodhidharma was exposed to as a young man; I am convinced he combined it with the Manichaean traditions of his family and so came up with the doctrines of Ch'an and Shaolin kung fu. We have seen that the martial arts were extant in China long before Bodhidharma arrived on the scene. His contribution, then, was to infuse them with both the ksatriya concept of martial spirituality and the Manichaean quest for inner light, and so develop a form of Buddhism that China had never seen: Ch'an and Shaolin kung fu.

John Chang tells us that Bodhidharma eventually completed all seventy-two levels of power and so managed union with the Absolute. He must have been something, since his legacy survives to the modern day.

There is one other semihistorical figure who bears notice, and who also reached the seventy-second level: Chang San Feng. An internal alchemist of great power, he is credited by many as the originator of the internal martial arts, that is to say the application of *nei dan* training to martial technique. John Chang's school of kung fu counts him as a prominent and highly successful member of its lineage. Among other things, Chang San Feng is believed by many to be the originator of t'ai chi chuan, although his alleged influence on t'ai chi is an area of controversy. Feng's name appears in historical Chinese texts under two different spellings, as Chang Three Mountain Peaks and Chang Three Abundances (both pronounced Chang San Feng). Some Chinese writers suggest that Chang lived to be at least five hundred years old or more.

The first reference we have of Chang is from the seventeenth-century scholar Huang Tsung-Hsi in his *Epitaph for Wang Cheng-nan*, who wrote:

Shaolin is famous for its martial art. However, their art stresses only offense, which allows an opponent to take advantage of this to strike weak points. There are Internal martial arts which employ stillness to overcome activeness; as soon as the aggressors come into bodily contact, they are immediately thrown. For this reason, Shaolin is regarded as an External martial art. The Internal martial arts originated with Chang San Feng (Chang Three Mountain Peaks) of the Sung dynasty (960-1279 C.E.), who was an alchemist on the mountain of Wu Tang. He received a summons from the emperor Hui Tsung. On the way to see the emperor, he found the road blocked by a group of bandits. That night he dreamed that the Heavenly Emperor Hsuan-Wu, the Taoist god of war, taught him martial arts. In the morning, Chang killed over a hundred bandits.[13]

Of significance is John's insistence that Chang was a Shaolin monk before he became a Taoist, something that fits in well with the seventeenth-century scholar Huang Pai-Chia's (Tsung-hsi's son's) statement that "Chang San Feng was a master of Shaolin, but reversing its principles developed the Internal school."[14] This is a distinction of some consequence to martial arts historians, one that has not been sufficiently stressed. Another important point is Huang's use of the word *stillness* (referring to yin energy) to describe internal martial arts. It must be noted that internal martial arts are not of necessity flowing and evasive, as we have come to believe in the West (since all movement is necessarily yang). Rather, Huang is denoting yin in the context used by John Chang—in other words as a gravitational force that absorbs energy and warps space-time. The *Epitaph for Wang Cheng-nan* offers considerable circumstantial evidence that John's school is indeed descended from Chang San Feng.

---

13. The wording is my own, based on two translations: Alfred Huang, *The Complete Tai Chi* (Tokyo: Charles E. Tuttle, 1993); Douglas Wile, *Lost T'ai-Chi Classics from the Late Ch'ing Dynasty* (Albany: SUNY Press, 1996).

14. Wile, *Lost T'ai-Chi Classics from the Late Ch'ing Dynasty*. I recommend this book to the serious scholar.

There is an additional indication in the name itself of John Chang's martial art, assuming that Chang San Feng truly was a monk at Shaolin. My teacher practices an art called Pa L'ei Chuan, or "Eight Ways Thunder Boxing." But the term *chuan* has rarely been translated correctly into English. It essentially means "shielded fist" or "clasped hands." One can see it in the salute given prior to and after the practice of Chinese martial arts: The left hand is clasped over the right fist, covering it, and the student bows to his teacher or his opponent. He is saying: "I am practicing a combative art but I am civilized—I will use it with discretion and refinement." One can also see the shielded fist in the following Chinese ideograms (figure 36).

Fig. 36. Chinese ideograms: *shou,* "hand" (right); *chuan,* "refined fist" (left)

On the right is the Chinese ideogram *shou* (*te,* in Japanese), which means "hand." Its Japanese form is used in the term *karate,* a word everyone knows, which means "empty hand." On the left is *chuan*— look carefully and you will see it portrays a "clasped hand," or, more appropriately, a "refined fist." The same meaning applies to *mukti* in the Sanskrit term vajramukti, which essentially means "thunderbolt clasped hands." Since *l'ei* means thunderbolt in Chinese, it is easy to see that L'ei Chuan is the Chinese translation of *vajramukti,* the martial art of the Indian ksatriya warrior nobility.

Now, Pa, when used by the Chinese, is usually a reference to the *pakua,* the eight directional patterns of the eight trigrams that make up the fundamental theories of Taoist doctrine. In essence, the pakua is Taoism. Beyond elementary translations and clarifications, then, Pa L'ei Chuan can also be construed to mean "the Taoist evolution of

Buddhist vajramukti." If Chang San Feng was truly a monk at Shaolin, as the legends indicate, then the name of John's school ties in well with his legacy.

Note 5. Hesychasm

Eastern mysticism distinguishes itself from Western by its conscious techniques of mind and body designed to give access to the mystical experience. These disciplines are akin to the Neoplatonist Plotinus's concern to be deaf to the sounds of the senses and keep the soul's faculty of apprehension one-pointed. Another example of Western physiological meditational techniques is the Hesychasts, a sect of Greek Orthodox mystics on Mt. Athos in the fourteenth century who used respiratory practices and concentration in conjunction with meditation and continual prayer to engage in a discipline later called the Jesus Prayer (the Greek word *hesychia* means "quiet"). St. John Climacus, a fifth-century monk and one of the greatest writers of the Hesychast tradition, wrote, "Let the remembrance of Jesus be present *with each breath*, and then you will know the value of the hesychia." In the late thirteenth century, St. Nicephorus the Hesychast produced an even more precise method of prayer, advising novices to "attach the prayer to their breathing" and to fix their eyes during prayer on the "middle of the body," in order to achieve a more total attention.[15]

Hesychasm was violently attacked in the first half of the fourteenth century by Barlaam the Calabrian, who called the Hesychasts *omphalopsychoi*, or "people having their souls in their navels." There were political connotations to the dispute, but theologically it centered on the question: Can man attain God through his own efforts? St. Gregory Palamas (1296–1359), a monk of Mt. Athos and later archbishop of Thessalonica, defended the Hesychast monks. In his view, the human body, sanctified by the sacraments of the church, is able to engage in the Jesus Prayer, and the devout may become able

15. Encyclopaedia Britannica Online, *Hesychasm*.

to see the "Uncreated Light" of Christ's Transfiguration that appeared on Mt. Tabor. This was a compromise in essence—yes, the psycho-physical (in essence yogic) practices of the Hesychasts were fine, but they worked only if sanctioned by the Church, and only through prayer to the Lord Jesus. Palamas's standpoint was that hesychasm prepared one for prayer, but that man ascended to God only through divine grace. Compromise or not, the teachings of Palamas were confirmed by the Orthodox Church in a series of councils held in Constantinople (1341, 1347, 1351). Hesychast spirituality is still practiced by Eastern Orthodox Christians and was once widely distributed throughout Russia after the publication of a collection of Hesychast writings, known as the *Philokalia*, in 1782.

APPENDIX 2:
The Red Shift
(Or, More Accurately,
Where I Eat Crow)

In *The Magus of Java*, I described seeing my master "energize" a Ping-Pong ball with yang ch'i as follows:

> John wanted to show me what the yang was like. It was night. He had just finished playing Ping-Pong with Johann, as they do every evening. Sifu took the Ping-Pong ball in his left hand and held it in the center of his palm. He opened his hands and held his right palm about two feet away. Suddenly the ball pulsed with bluish violet light; it made a noise, too, sort of like a canary singing. Bluish white sparks flew from the ball toward his right palm; they were like miniature lightning bolts. He kept it up for a few seconds and then handed me the ball. It wasn't overly hot, but it was warm. I did my usual thing and cut it in half on the spot, which pissed everybody off, because it was the last ball in the house and they wanted to continue their game. But I had to make sure that there wasn't any circuitry inside the ball."[1]

---

1. *The Magus of Java*, p. 102.

Everything about the depiction above is correct, except for the color. The actual color of the ball during the demonstration was red.

While at rest it is blue (and in its purest form becomes white), it seems that the yang ch'i actually changes color when in opposition to the yin and turns red. (Hence, in the ta'i ch'i symbol, the color of the yang should be red.) I call this change *the red shift*. What I managed to do in the course of events was trick myself into believing something other than what I had actually seen.

How did this come about? When I first witnessed this demonstration, I had seen the ball pulse with a red light. I then asked John, thinking of the heat as I did so: "Sifu, is the color of the yang ch'i red?"

"No," he replied, "it's blue."

That short-circuited a few fuses as I began to doubt my own eyes. I had seen it to be red!

This incident troubled me for years, but I did not want to doubt my teacher's say-so. While writing *The Magus of Java* (actually toward the final editing), I was privileged to see a demonstration of the "lightning bolts" John is capable of issuing—in essence, energy blasts. They were bluish white. In the meantime I had read the available literature, and everyone from Hindu yogis to Wilhelm Reich himself had made reference to bioenergy being blue. *That clinches it*, I thought, after seeing the energy-blast demo, *I need my eyes checked*. And so I called the yang ch'i in the Ping-Pong ball demo bluish violet, a wishy-washy compromise between what I thought I had seen and what I had been told I had seen.

Well, I was wrong to do so, and I apologize. These books of mine stretch the imagination and my credibility as it is; if they are indeed to be phenomenological reports, then I should be absolutely convinced of everything I put down on paper. Since that time I have seen both demos again; the red shift exists and it is very real. On the other hand, the yang ch'i is indeed blue when unopposed by the yin.

How this works is simple: While my teacher's "lightning bolts" are in fact yin-yang kung—that is to say they inherently have both yin and yang energies—the yin is passive when used in this manner, as it is in nature. The yin simply follows the yang, in other words. Whether this means that yang ch'i is blue when followed by (in contact with, but unopposed by) the yin ch'i, or is blue of its own accord, I do not know, and John will not say. Indeed, he added one more conundrum to the situation by stating, when queried, that "in its purest form the yang ch'i is white." It would seem that the color of the yang ch'i, then, can range from red to blue to purest white.

Another area I would like to clarify, about which I have been questioned by many readers, is the point of the two dots of opposing energy inherent in the classic t'ai chi symbol. In other words, in *The Magus of Java* I used this symbol to describe t'ai-chi:

while most people are used to this one:

The common explanation for the second, more popular symbol is that "there is a little yang in the purest yin, a little yin in the purest yang." Another way of stating it would be "there is a little bad in the best of us, a little good in the worst of us." Such a statement implies a distribution of proportions, however, and this is not the case for t'ai-chi—yin has no yang in it, nor does yang contain yin. In *The Magus of Java* I did my best to get the message across that yin and yang are *opposing*, not complementary, forces; this is the reason that I insisted on the first, rather than the latter, symbol. The classic image that many people have of yang flowing harmoniously into yin is erroneous; this is something the reader *must* comprehend, even though many teachers in China today may say otherwise. Without my risking giving away the secrets of our school, I will say this as clarification: What the "classic" t'ai chi symbol means is that *the seeds of yin are contained within an abundance of yang, while the seeds of yang within an abundance of yin.* Consider the macrocosmic example of a red giant star spontaneously collapsing into a black hole, and you will have a good idea of what the two dots mean.

In short, we are talking about a spontaneous reversion following a massive aggregation. For example, recent investigations in astrophysics seem to indicate that galaxies are created by the "seeding" of supermassive black holes in their center (in short, an abundance of yin creating the beginnings of yang). It is interesting to note that the galaxies in question also evidence the ellipsoidal curvature indicated by the classic t'ai chi symbol.[2] Buddhist doctrine would say "emptiness is form and form is emptiness" by way of explanation, but this transition is neither smooth nor painless—birth and death never are, you see. The ancient Chinese, who knew nothing of black holes and red giants, discovered these truisms by turning within. I will say no more, but end hoping that what I have elaborated on here will serve my readers as an apology for my earlier faux pas.

---

2. For example, the black hole in the center of the Andromeda galaxy has a mass thirty million times that of our sun. Black holes are found only in the center of galaxies that evidence ellipsoidal "bumps" in their center, such as our own and the Andromeda galaxy.

BOOKS OF RELATED INTEREST

THE MAGUS OF JAVA
Teachings of an Authentic Taoist Immortal
by Kosta Danaos

RING OF FIRE
An Indonesian Odyssey
by Lawrence Blair with Lorne Blair

MARTIAL AARTS TEACHING TALES OF POWER AND PARADOX
Freeing the Mind, Focusing Chi, and Mastering the Self
by Pascal Fauliot

THE SPIRITUAL FOUNDATIONS OF AIKIDO
by William Gleason

ORIGINAL WISDOM
Stories of an Ancient Way of Knowing
by Robert Wolff

OTHER WAYS OF KNOWING
Recharting Our Future with Ageless Wisdom
by John Broomfield

QIGONG TEACHINGS OF A TAOIST IMMORTAL
The Eight Essential Exercises of Master Li Ching-yun
by Stuart Alve Olson

THE WARRIOR IS SILENT
Martial Arts and the Spiritual Path
Scott Shaw, Ph.D.

Inner Traditions • Bear & Company
P.O. Box 388
Rochester, VT 05767
1-800-246-8648
www.InnerTraditions.com

Or contact your local bookseller